THE ONTARIO
BUTTERFLY ATLAS

ANTHONY M. HOLMES

QUIMBY F. HESS *Quimby F. Hess*

RONALD R. TASKER

ALAN J. HANKS

Canadian Cataloging in Publication Data

Main entry under title:

The Ontario butterfly atlas

Includes index
ISBN 0-921631-11-1

1. Butterflies — Ontario.   I. Holmes, Anthony M.,
1930-   .   II. Toronto Entomologists Association.

QL552.057 1991   595.78'9'09713   C91-095753-3

©1991 Toronto Entomologists' Association , 34 Seaton Drive, Aurora, Ont.,
Toronto, Ontario   L4G 2K1

Printed in Canada
by D.W. Friesen
Altona, Manitoba
R0G 0B0
Canada

Front Cover Photo:
The Old World Swallowtail (*Papilio machaon hudsonianus*) female near
Geraldton, Ontario (Thunder Bay Dist.) on June 22, 1971.

PREFACE

Despite the importance of the Province of Ontario it is one of the few Canadian Provinces which does not yet have a comprehensive publication dealing with the butterfly fauna. The main objective of this Ontario Butterfly Atlas is to provide a concise, authoritative and complete record of occurrence and distribution of the butterflies of Ontario for the use of professional and amateur entomologists and those others who might be interested in our butterfly fauna.

This is particularly important at this time since many habitats are threatened by development and land use changes. Some species are in need of urgent conservation measures.

Much of the data presented is based on the findings of various members of the Toronto Entomologists' Association (T.E.A.), formed in 1969 with the encouragement of the staff of the Department of Entomology of the Royal Ontario Museum and, in particular, Research Associate J.C.E. Riotte, M.A. These findings have been published in Seasonal Summaries for a number of years.

We wish to acknowledge the assistance and cooperation of all those whose contributions have made this Atlas a reality. Apart from the various contributors to the TEA publications, we are grateful for the help and encouragement received from the staff of the Royal Ontario Museum over the years. Encouragement was also received from the Ministry of Natural Resources and, in particular, Dr. J. MacLean and Irene Bowman of the Wildlife Policy Research Branch. In addition, we acknowledge the assistance provided by the Federation of Ontario Naturalists, the World Wildlife Fund, the Ontario Heritage Foundation, the McLean Foundation and the Nature Conservancy of Canada, especially Michelle Woulfe and Sheila McKay.

Figure 3 is taken from "The Atlas of the Breeding Birds of Ontario", by kind permission of the Federation of Ontario Naturalists.

Photographs were very kindly contributed by the following individuals: Alan J. Hanks; Quimby F. Hess; Brenda Kulon (Karner Blue larva on page 108); Alan L. Patterson (The Dainty Sulphur — page 76); Walter Plath Jr., Tim Sabo, Jim Spottiswood and Ronald R. Tasker.

Anthony M. Holmes
Ronald R. Tasker

Quimby F. Hess
Alan J. Hanks

THE AUTHORS

Anthony Holmes: has been interested in Lepidoptera and an amateur entomologist for over 40 years. He has studied and collected in Europe, southern Africa and eastern Canada. He was instrumental in the creation of, and is a founding member of the Toronto Entomologists' Association. Much of the base work for this endeavour was compiled by him from the early records. Among other claims to fame was the discovery in 1950 of a new species of butterfly, *Thestor holmesi* Van Son, in the eastern Cape Province of South Africa.

Quimby Hess: has observed and studied butterflies in Ontario for sixty years. As a Forester, he worked on the Forest Insect Survey in northern Ontario and has done field work on Lepidoptera over most of the province and in northern Manitoba and the N.W. Territories. He has also studied extensively in the United States and in Central and South America. He has since 1972 been responsible for compiling the Annual Summaries of the Toronto Entomologists' Association and has thus gained an extensive knowledge of the distribution of Ontario butterflies and contributed significantly to the material given here. In 1967 he was awarded the Centennial Medal by the Government of Canada for service to the nation.

Ronald Tasker: has made a hobby of natural history all his life, having been a member of the executive of the Federation of Ontario Naturalists, a trustee of the Nature Conservancy of Canada and Chairman of the Board of the Long Point Bird Observatory. With a particular interest in Lepidoptera he has done extensive work on the butterflies of Manitoulin Island in Ontario, particularly in helping to determine the correct status of a number of the rare species.

Alan Hanks: has collected and studied butterflies in both England and Canada and has been secretary/treasurer of the Toronto Entomologists' Association for the last eighteen years. In collaboration with Quimby Hess, he has played a significant part in the production of the Annual Summaries. He was the recipient of the Entomological Society of Canada Norman Criddle Award for 1982-83.

CONTENTS

FIGURES

INTRODUCTION

The purpose of this Atlas is essentially three-fold:

* To summarize what is presently known about the distribution and some characteristics of Ontario's butterflies,
* To encourage lepidopterists and others who may be interested in further study to explore the distribution of Ontario butterflies,
* To provide a reference for planning efforts to conserve our rarer species and those that are in danger of extirpation.

Until the late 1960's little had been systematically recorded concerning the distribution and life history of Ontario's butterflies. There were a number of lists, notably those of Bethune, Bailey and Riotte, as well as notes on occurrences in particular locations or small areas in the province, but little in the way of a province-wide study. Subsequently, the Toronto Entomologists' Association has provided a focus for assembling further occurrence data through members and other contributions to the Seasonal Summaries. These activities have yielded a vast amount of new distribution data, producing a need for systematic organization. By doing this the gaps in our knowledge were revealed and those wishing to contribute to filling these gaps are provided with some direction. Furthermore, efforts are needed to ensure that our rare butterflies, several of which are in danger of disappearing, remain with us.

In assembling this Atlas, we have tried to be brief, and avoid duplication of the available literature.

TORONTO ENTOMOLOGISTS' ASSOCIATION

In September of 1967 a group of amateur entomologists gathered for an open air lunch in High Park, Toronto. The initiative came from staff of the Dept. of Entomology of the Royal Ontario Museum, in particular Research Associate J.C.E. Riotte and Dept. Secretary Isobel Smyth. Together with some half dozen other dedicated amateurs this group formed the local branch of the Michigan Entomological Society, calling it the Toronto Branch. With increased activity and a growth in membership in the spring of 1970 an independent association was decided on - the Toronto Entomologists' Association.

The association now has some 80 members and has published a Seasonal Summary each year since its formation. It works particularly to further knowledge of Ontario insects, especially butterflies, and is extremely concerned with matters of conservation. Through these efforts it promotes awareness of the need to preserve habitats and has made successful representations to the Provincial Government to have several rare and threatened species listed as endangered.

NOMENCLATURE

With respect to nomenclature, we have followed "A Catalogue/Checklist of the Butterflies of North America North of Mexico" by Lee D. Miller and F.M. Brown (The Lepidopterist's Society Memoir No. 2 -1981) and the "Supplement to A Catalogue/Checklist of the Butterflies of North America North of Mexico" by Clifford D. Ferris (The Lepidopterist's Society Memoir No. 3, 1989).

TIMETABLES

Apart from dates during which the adults fly, surprisingly little is known about Ontario's butterfly timetables although hibernation has been recorded in some detail by Scott (1979). With the exception of Scudder (1889), who wrote almost a century ago, the literature has tended to neglect the early life history stages. Nevertheless, a good deal may be conjectured; even so, the timetables given here should be regarded as tentative. For example, it is evident that for a number of species, southern Ontario is an area where multiple broods give way to single ones.

HABITAT

Descriptions of the habitats in which the butterflies are found has been kept brief as existing literature gives much useful information. The notes included herein are intended merely as a guide to the reader as to where to look for a particular species.

Distributions are provided visually by the use of maps. Although only actual records are illustrated, for most species this gives a reasonably good idea of the current state of knowledge about distribution.

STATUS

The symbols given to represent the status for each species are taken from a report made to the Ontario Heritage Foundation by the Nature Conservancy of Canada. It attempts to introduce a degree of objectivity into the question of abundance for wildlife in general by providing a series of defined terms which may be applied to individual species. The definitions and their application as modified by us for the butterflies, are given in a later section.

RECORDS

The records presented in this Atlas are drawn mainly from the published lists and summaries noted in the Bibliography, supplemented by data from the Royal Ontario Museum, the Canadian National Collection and several private collections. Although time constraints have precluded a complete search of museum specimens, most of the localities whence museum specimens were obtained have also been reported in the literature so that it is unlikely that critical occurrence data have been missed. Locations of counties and districts mentioned in describing distributions are shown on Figures 1 and 2.

While the inclusion of published records rather than a reliance on actual verified extant specimens may raise questions of authenticity this is not considered a problem. It is unlikely that there are many mis-identifications or doubtful records among the included species except where noted in the text and the few that have been introduced are unlikely to alter the distribution as illustrated.

The main body of the text lists all butterfly species presently known to be continuously resident within the boundaries of Ontario, as well as those migrants which make reasonably frequent visits. One or two visitors such as *B. philenor* and *E. claudia*, though they tend to be infrequent, have occurred often enough historically to warrant recognition as sometime Ontario butterflies.

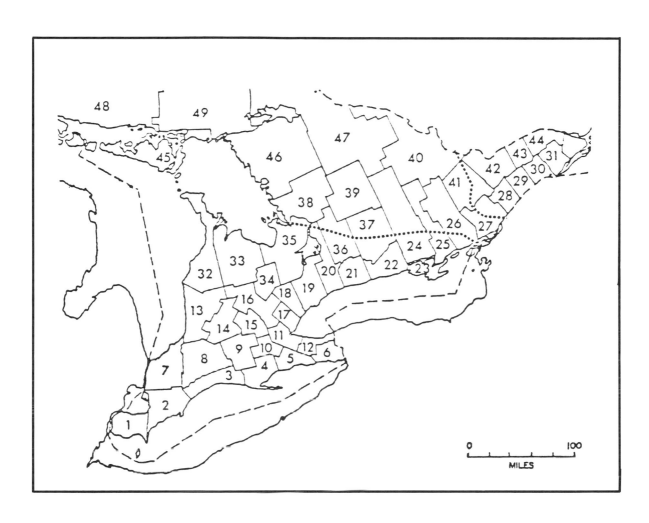

ALGOMA	48	HALDIMAND	5	MIDDLESEX	8	PRINCE EDWARD	23
BRANT	10	HALIBURTON	39	MUSKOKA	38	RENFREW	40
BRUCE	32	HALTON	17	NIPISSING	47	RUSSELL	43
CARLETON	42	HASTINGS	24	NORFOLK	4	SIMCOE	35
DUFFERIN	34	HURON	13	NORTHUMBERLAND	22	STORMONT	30
DUNDAS	29	KENT	2	ONTARIO	20	SUDBURY	49
DURHAM	21	LAMBTON	7	OXFORD	9	VICTORIA	36
ELGIN	3	LANARK	41	PARRY SOUND	46	WATERLOO	15
ESSEX	1	LEEDS	27	PEEL	18	WELLAND	6
FRONTENAC	26	LENNOX		PERTH	14	WELLINGTON	16
GLENGARRY	31	& ADDINGTON	25	PETERBOROUGH	37	WENTWORTH	11
GRENVILLE	28	LINCOLN	12	PRESCOTT	44	YORK	19
GREY	33	MANITOULIN	45				

NOTE: The following are combined now into Regional Municipalities:
Hamilton & Wentworth; Lincoln & Welland (Niagara); Haldimand & Norfolk; Carleton is Ottawa-Carleton. The dotted line represents Shield limits.

FIGURE 1. COUNTIES & DISTRICTS OF SOUTHERN ONTARIO

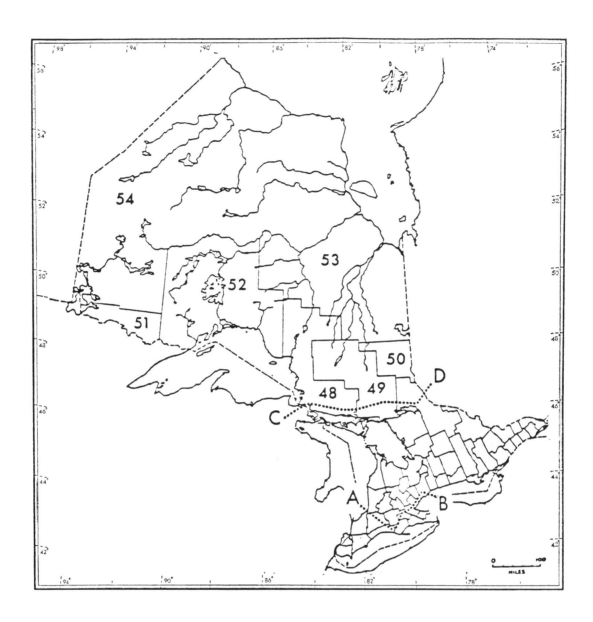

ALGOMA	48	SUDBURY	49
COCHRANE	53	THUNDER BAY	52
KENORA	54	TIMISKAMING	50
RAINY RIVER	51		

NOTE: The line A-B represents the approximate northern limits of the Carolinian Zone in Ontario. Line C-D approximates the 40F mean daily temperature for the year isotherm, and has been adopted here as the northern limit of southern Ontario.

FIGURE 2. DISTRICTS OF NORTHERN ONTARIO

Following this is a listing of strays, unconfirmed or doubtful species. Some of these may occasionally be swept into the province as a result of fall hurricanes or otherwise wander far north or east of their normal ranges. Others are unconfirmed as residents or else the authenticity of their occurrence is in doubt.

PHYSIOGRAPHIC FEATURES

The Province of Ontario is located in central Canada and extends from the shores of Hudson and James Bays south to the Great Lakes, east to the Ottawa River and the boundary with Quebec and west to Lake of the Woods and the boundary with Manitoba. It is usually divided into northern and southern regions, the boundary between these taken here as being from the mouth of the French River through Lake Nipissing to Mattawa (see line C-D on Figure 2).
There are two main watersheds in Ontario - the Arctic and Atlantic Watersheds. All of Ontario was glaciated during the last Ice Age which started retreating from Lake Erie some 14,000 years ago.

The major physiographic features in Ontario from north to south are as follows:

a) **The Hudson Bay Lowlands** - a vast region whose climate and drainage has produced a large expanse of continuously waterlogged land which occupies one-quarter of the surface area of Ontario - approximately 64,000,000 acres.

b) **The Canadian Shield region** - a large area with a great deal of exposed rock and many lakes, and including a tongue (known as the Frontenac Axis) extending to the St. Lawrence River in the vicinity of Kingston.

c) **The Great Lakes/St. Lawrence region** - this occupies most of southern Ontario.

The forest regions of Ontario include the following:

a) **Sub-arctic tundra** - this extends along the coast of Hudson Bay and includes permafrost areas.

b) **Boreal forest region** - extending southwards from the sub-arctic tundra to the Great Lakes/St. Lawrence region.

c) **Great Lakes/St. Lawrence region** - this is south of the boreal forest region and extends from the Algoma District easterly to the Quebec border near Lake Temiskaming and southwards to the deciduous forest region.

d) **Deciduous forest region** - this is in southwestern Ontario between Lakes Huron, Erie and Ontario.

These features are shown on Figure 3.

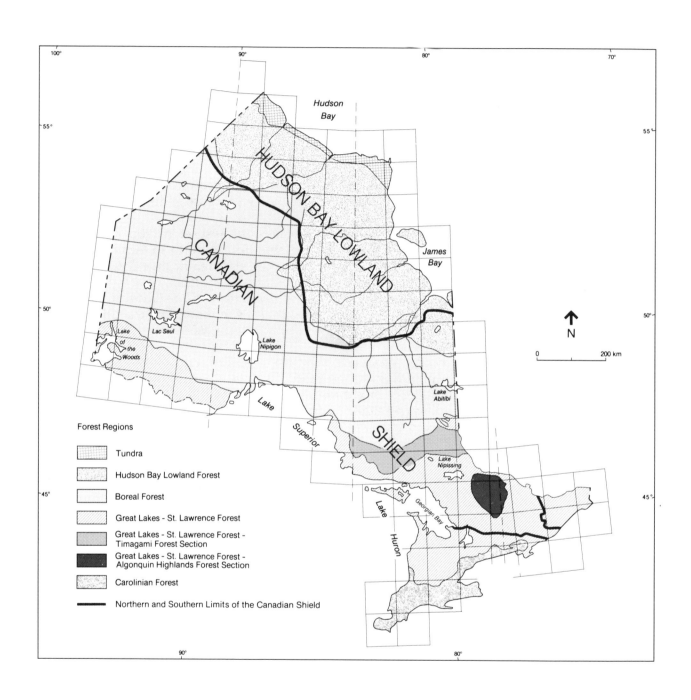

Forest Regions

Tundra

Hudson Bay Lowland Forest

Boreal Forest

Great Lakes - St. Lawrence Forest

Great Lakes - St. Lawrence Forest - Timagami Forest Section

Great Lakes - St. Lawrence Forest - Algonquin Highlands Forest Section

Carolinian Forest

Northern and Southern Limits of the Canadian Shield

FIGURE 3. PHYSIOGRAPHIC AND FOREST FEATURES OF ONTARIO.

LIFE ZONES

Ontario includes four life zones, deriving to some extent from the physiographic features; the Hudsonian, Canadian, Transition and Carolinian, as shown on Figure 4 (after Klots). They are characterized by associations of plants and animals and certain assemblages of butterflies are typical of each.

The Hudsonian Zone is a borderline area between the arctic and northern forest. In Ontario this zone occupies the Hudson Bay Lowlands extending inland about 200 miles from the shore. The vegetation is characterized by an almost endless tract of black spruce and tamarack muskeg in which the typical butterflies are those of the sub-arctic such as *Colias gigantea*, *C. pelidne* and *C. palaeno*, those coming in from the adjacent northern forest such as the skipper *Pyrgus centaureae*, and bog species such as *Clossiana frigga* and *Oeneis jutta*. Apart from very limited records from a few points along the shore, the butterfly population of this area is poorly known because of the difficulty of access.

The Canadian Zone consists of the typical northern coniferous forest set in a topography of rock outcrops and lakes extending from the Hudson Bay Lowlands in the north to Georgian Bay and the St. Lawrence Valley in the south. Butterfly species typifying the area include *Papilio glaucus*, *P. machaon*, *Euchloe ausonides*, *Colias interior*; several blues such as *Everes amyntula*, *Glaucopsyche lygdamus*, *Lycaeides idas* and *Plebejus saepiolus*; fritillaries such as *Clossiana eunomia*, *C. freija* and *C. titania*; the nymphalids *Polygonia faunus*, *Nymphulis vau-album* and *Basilarchia a. arthemis* and the satyrids *Erebia disa*, *E. discoidalis*, *Oeneis macounii*, *O. chryxus* and *Coenonympha inornata*.

The Transition Zone, like the Hudsonian, is a borderline area between the northern coniferous forest and the more southerly deciduous forest. It occupies a relatively narrow band across southern Ontario, its natural vegetation consisting of mixed forest much of which has now been replaced by agriculture. The butterfly fauna is drawn mainly from the adjacent areas and few, if any, species are confined to the zone. Typical species include *Pieris virginiensis*, the hairstreaks *Satyrium edwardsii*, *S. calanus* and *S. caryaevorum*, and *Euphydryas phaeton*.

The Carolinian Zone occupies only a narrow portion of southwestern Ontario along the shorelines of Lakes Erie, Ontario and Huron. Some disjunct Carolinian elements are found towards the eastern end of Lake Ontario where some Carolinian butterflies are also found. Typical are the skippers *Atrytone logan*, *Euphyes dion* and *E. conspicua* and the swallowtails *Heraclides cresphontes* and *Papilio troilus*. This zone in Ontario is on the northern fringe of a much larger area stretching south to the Carolinas with a rich butterfly fauna. A number of species found in the southern parts of the province are on the northern edge of their range and are subject to periodic range expansions and contractions.

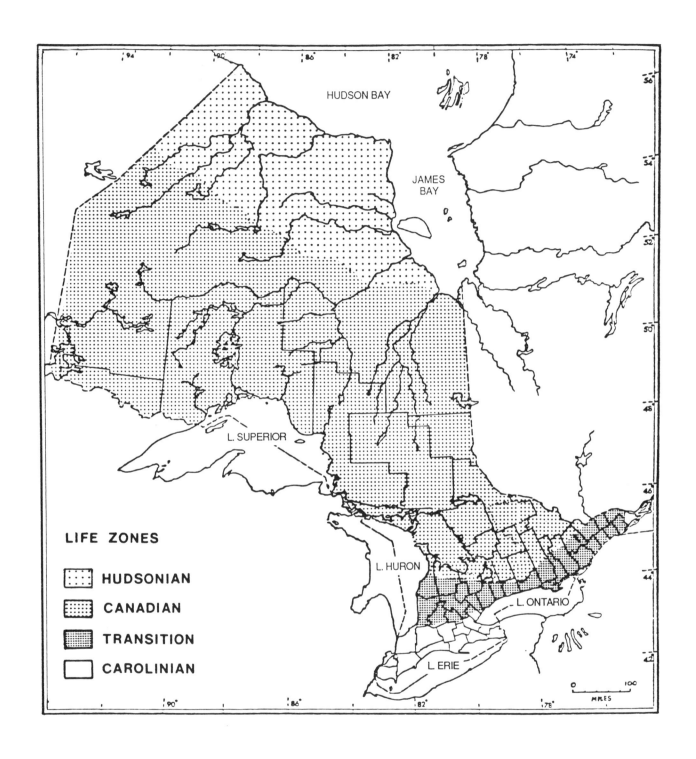

LIFE ZONES

- :::: HUDSONIAN
- ▦ CANADIAN
- ▤ TRANSITION
- ☐ CAROLINIAN

FIGURE 4. LIFE ZONES IN ONTARIO

8

PROBLEM SPECIES

With the exception of *Basilarchia arthemis astyanax* and *B.a.arthemis*, which are different butterflies to most peoples' eyes, we have not attempted to differentiate sub-species except in a few cases. The prime reason for this is that they are not often enough distinguished in the historical records, particularly older ones.

Several butterflies are treated as species by some authors and sub-species by others. Thus *Enodia anthedon* is sometimes regarded as a separate species and sometimes as a subspecies of *E. portlandia*. All records for both names have been included under *E. anthedon*. Similarly with *Satyrodes fumosa* and *S. eurydice*, recorded here as *S. eurydice*, and *S. appalachia*.

Some members of the genera *Erynnis* and *Satyrium* are difficult to separate into species so that some records may be inaccurate because of this. A number of skippers, including *Staphylus hayhurstii, Oarisma garita* and *Atrytonopsis hianna* are presently known from only one or two locations in Ontario; although their habitats are not known to be endangered, their needs must be respected if they are to continue to survive in the province. On the other hand, some species may be more plentiful than yet realized. The recent identification of *Pieris virginiensis* in several widely spread localities when it was once believed to be restricted to one locality near Hamilton, underlines the need for more intensive investigations.

* * * * * * * * * * * * * * * * * * *

Grassy lakeshore in jackpine forest near Munro Lake (Munro Twp. Cochrane Dist.) with Bog Goldenrod, nectar source for the Purple Lesser Fritillary (*Clossiana titania*) in August, 1980.

Bog with grass, sphagnum and dwarf black spruce in McCoig Twp. (Cochrane Dist.) west of Hearst. The Jutta Arctic, Bog Fritillary, Saga Fritillary, Red-Disked Alpine and Brown Elfin have all been found here.

Family: HESPERIIDAE

The Skipper Butterflies

Juvenal's Dusky Wing (*Erynnis juvenalis*) at St. Williams, June 2, 1974.

The Least Skipper (*Ancyloxypha numitor*) in the Dundas Valley, August 26, 1974.

The Tawny Edged Skipper (*Polites themistocles*) at Freelton, July 6, 1975.

SPECIES: *Epargyreus clarus* (Cramer)   Silver Spotted Skipper

TIMETABLE:

Apr.	May	June	July	Aug.	Sep.	Oct.
Pupa---------						
	Adult-----------					
			Eggs--------			
				Larva----------------------		
						Pupa---------

Broods   One.

Hibernates   As a pupa.

OCCURRENCE:

Habitat   Gardens, roadsides and the edges of woods, especially where there are flowers.

Food Plant   Various legumes, especially locust, wisteria, false indigo.

Distribution Widespread and sometimes locally common, mainly south of the Shield and reported from one location near Lake of the Woods.

Status   S3

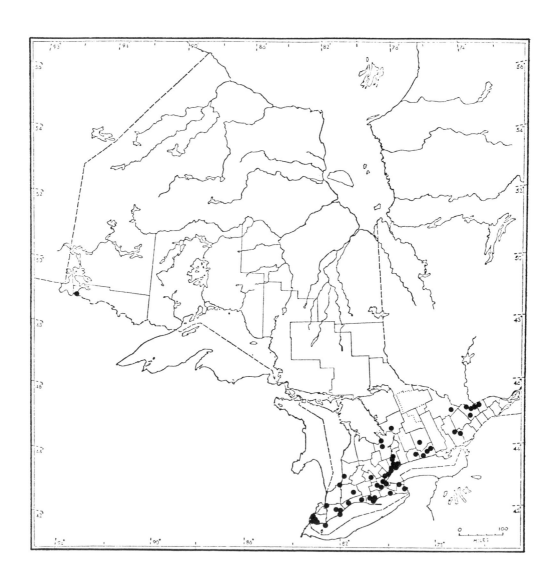

SPECIES: *Thorybes bathyllus* (J.E. Smith)

TIMETABLE:

Broods   One.

Hibernates   As a mature larva.

OCCURRENCE:

Habitat   Fields, open spaces and roadsides.

Food Plant   Various legumes, especially beggar's tick.

Distribution   Apparently rare and local, found only in the southerly parts of the province.

Status   S2

Southern Cloudy Wing

Apr.	May	June	July	Aug.	Sep.	Oct.
Larvae------------						
		Pupa				
		Adult--------				
			Eggs			
			Larva---------------------			

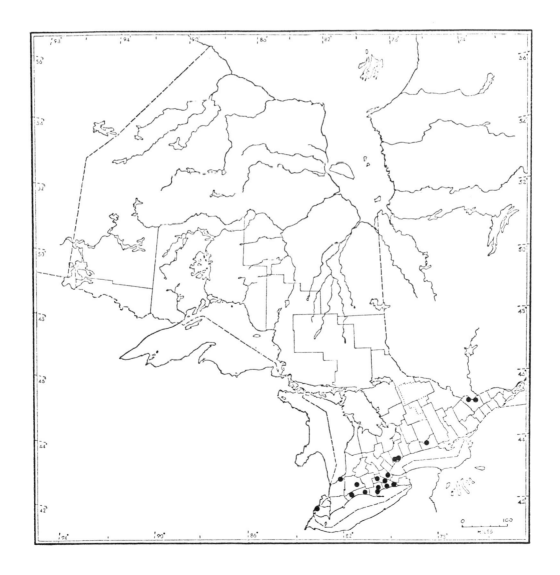

SPECIES: *Thorybes pylades* (Scudder)

Northern Cloudy Wing

TIMETABLE:

Broods — Usually one, but there there may be a partial second in the south.

Hibernates — As a mature larva.

Apr.	May	June	July	Aug.	Sep.	Oct.
Larva--------						
	Pupa-------					
	Adult---------					
	Eggs--					
	Larva--------------------------------					
Some:			Pupa			
			Adult			
			Eggs			
			Larva------------			

OCCURRENCE:

Habitat — Fields, open spaces and roadsides.

Food Plant — Various legumes, especially clovers, tick-trefoil, milk vetch and alfalfa.

Distribution — Widespread and sometimes common over almost the whole province, but not presently known from the Hudson Bay Lowlands.

Status — S5

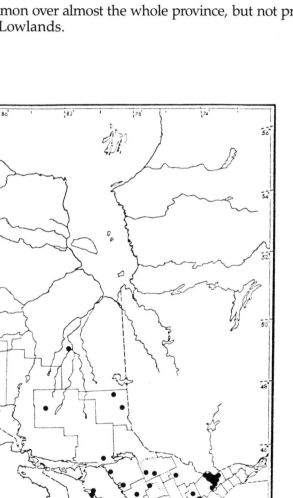

SPECIES: *Staphylus hayhurstii* (W.H. Edwards)

Southern Sooty Wing

TIMETABLE:

Broods   Probably two but this needs substantiation for Ontario.

Hibernates   As a larva.

OCCURRENCE:

Habitat   Roadsides and trails near woodlands.

Food Plant   Lamb's quarters.

Distribution   Recently discovered in the province, so far only recorded from Point Pelee and Pelee Island.

Status   S3

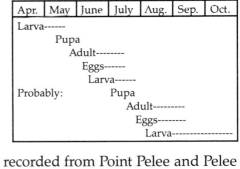

Apr.	May	June	July	Aug.	Sep.	Oct.
Larva------						
	Pupa					
		Adult--------				
			Eggs------			
			Larva------			
Probably:		Pupa				
			Adult---------			
			Eggs--------			
				Larva----------------		

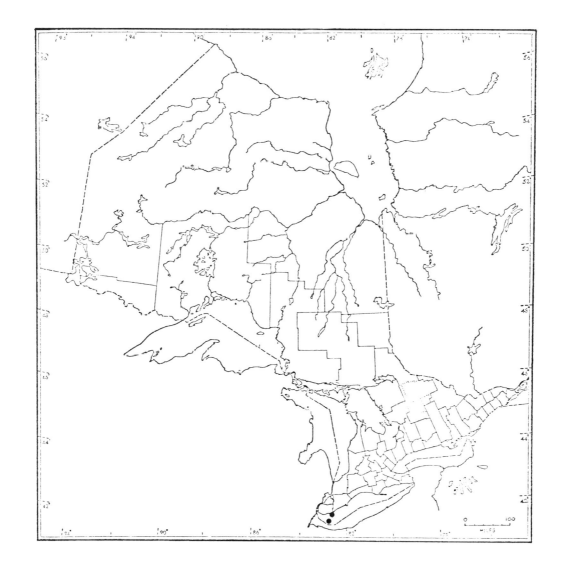

15

SPECIES: *Erynnis icelus* (Scudder & Burgess)   Dreamy Dusky Wing

TIMETABLE:

Apr.	May	June	July	Aug.	Sep.	Oct.
Larva----------						
	Pupa--------					
	Adult-----------					
		Eggs------				
		Larva-------------------------------				

Broods   One

Hibernates   As a mature larva.

OCCURRENCE:

Habitat   Fields, open spaces, roadsides and woodland trails.

Food Plant   Willows, poplars, aspens and birch.

Distribution   Widespread and common over almost all the province and recorded north into the
                Hudson Bay Lowlands.

Status   S5

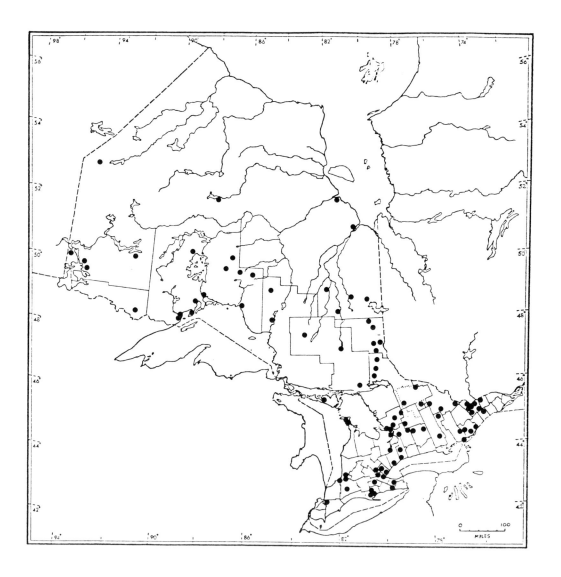

SPECIES: *Erynnis brizo* (Boisduval & Leconte)   Sleepy Dusky Wing

TIMETABLE:

Broods   One.

Hibernates   As a mature larva.

Apr.	May	June	July	Aug.	Sep.	Oct.
Larva--------						
	Pupa------					
		Adult-------				
		Eggs				
			Larva----------------------------			

OCCURRENCE:

Habitat   Open spaces, roadsides and woodland trails.

Food Plant   Various species of oak.

Distribution Widespread over the southerly parts of the province, and recorded as far north as Sudbury.

Status   S4

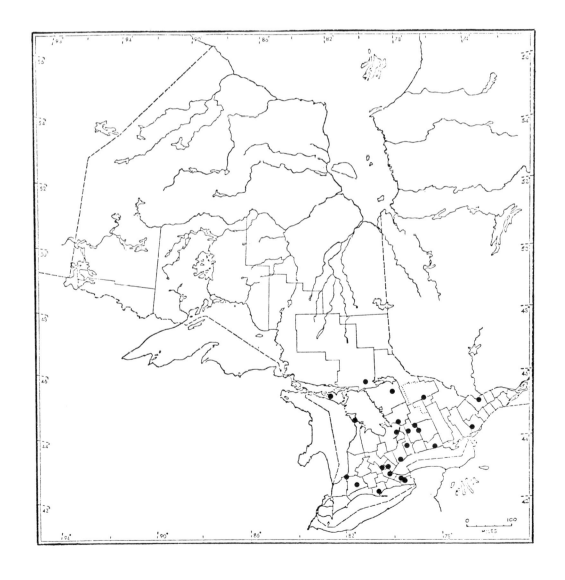

SPECIES: *Erynnis juvenalis* (Fabricius)

Juvenal's Dusky Wing

TIMETABLE:

Apr.	May	June	July	Aug.	Sep.	Oct.
Larva----						
	Pupa					
	Adult-----------					
		Eggs------				
		Larva---------------------------------				
Some:			Pupa			
			Adult----			
			Eggs			
				Larva--------		

Broods   Usually one, but there may be a partial second in the south.

Hibernates   As a mature larva.

OCCURRENCE:

Habitat   Mainly open woods with oak, but also fields, open spaces and roadsides, especially near woodlands.

Food Plant   Various species of oak.

Distribution Widespread and common over the southerly parts of the province, also recorded from the north shore of Lake Superior and Lake of the Woods.

Status   S5

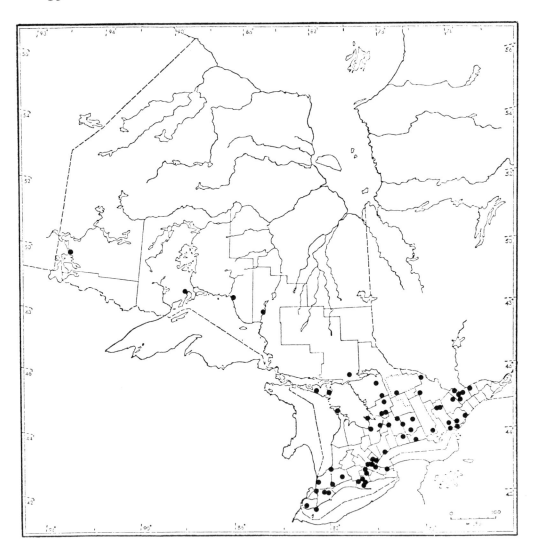

SPECIES: *Erynnis horatius* (Scudder & Burgess)   Horace's Dusky Wing

TIMETABLE:

Apr.	May	June	July	Aug.	Sep.	Oct.
Larva----						
	Pupa					
		Adult--				
		Eggs				
			Larva----			
				Pupa		
				Adult		
					Eggs--	
						Larva---------------

Broods   Two.

Hibernates   As a larva.

OCCURRENCE:

Habitat   Sandy pine and oak woods.

Food Plant   Various species of oak.

Distribution   Rare, recorded only from Pinery Park, St. Williams, Point Pelee and Northumberland County.

Status   S2

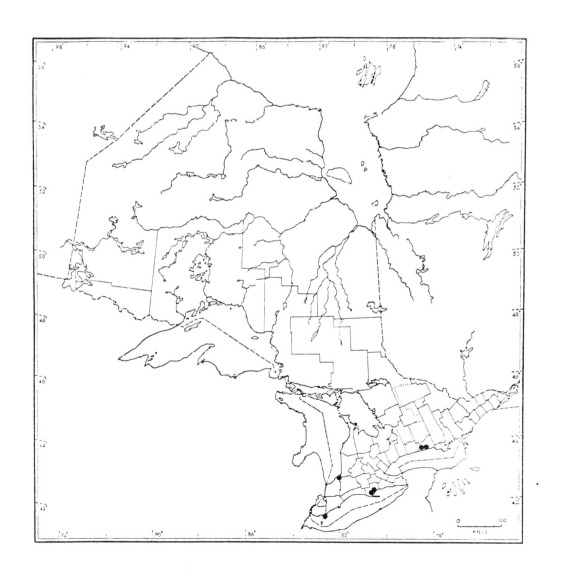

19

SPECIES: *Erynnis martialis* (Scudder)   Mottled Dusky Wing

TIMETABLE:

Apr.	May	June	July	Aug.	Sep.	Oct.
Larva-----						
	Pupa					
		Adult---				
		Eggs---				
			Larva----------			
Probably:			Pupa			
				Adult---		
				Eggs---		
					Larva-----------------	

Broods   Probably two, but this needs substantiation for Ontario.

Hibernates   As a mature larva.

OCCURRENCE:

Habitat   Oak savannah and sandy areas with New Jersey tea.

Food Plant   New Jersey tea.

Distribution   Rare, found only in the southerly parts of the province.

Status   S3

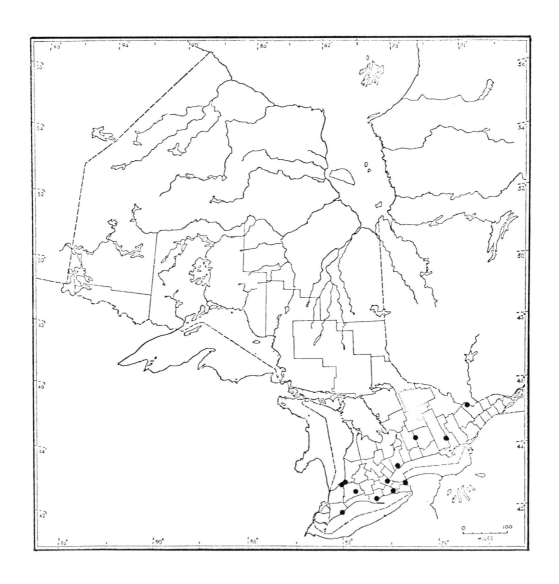

SPECIES: *Erynnis lucilius* (Scudder & Burgess)   Columbine Dusky Wing

TIMETABLE:

Broods   Usually one, but there may be a partial second.

Hibernates   As a mature larva.

OCCURRENCE:

Habitat   Open spaces, roadsides and woodland trails.

Food Plant   Wild columbine.

Distribution   Widespread and fairly common as far north as
                Manitoulin Island and Algonquin Park.

Status   S5

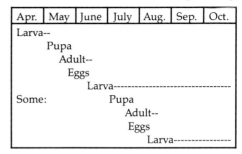

Apr.	May	June	July	Aug.	Sep.	Oct.
Larva--						
	Pupa					
		Adult--				
		Eggs				
			Larva------------------------------			
Some:			Pupa			
				Adult--		
				Eggs		
					Larva--------------	

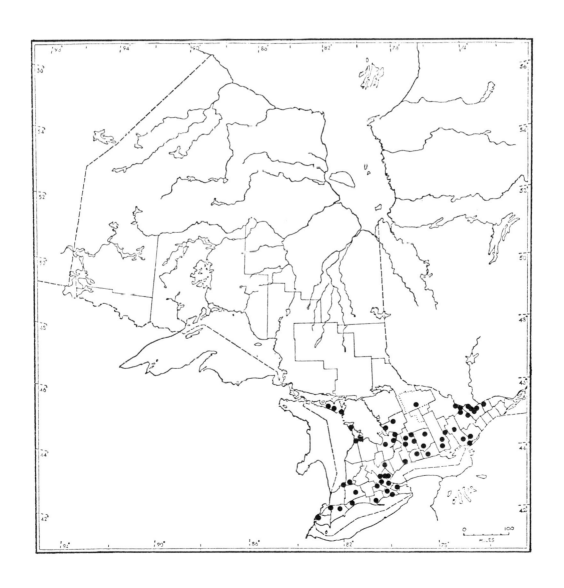

21

SPECIES: *Erynnis baptisiae* (Forbes)   Wild Indigo Dusky Wing

TIMETABLE:

Apr.	May	June	July	Aug.	Sep.	Oct.
Larva---------						
	Pupa					
	Adult					
		Eggs				
		Larva				
		Pupa				
			Adult			
			Eggs			
				Larva--------------------		

Broods   Two.

Hibernates   As a mature larva.

OCCURRENCE:

Habitat   Fields, open spaces and roadsides.

Food Plant   Pea family, usually wild indigo, other indigos or wild lupine.

Distribution   Rare and very local, recorded only near Windsor, Walpole Island and St. Williams.

Status   S2

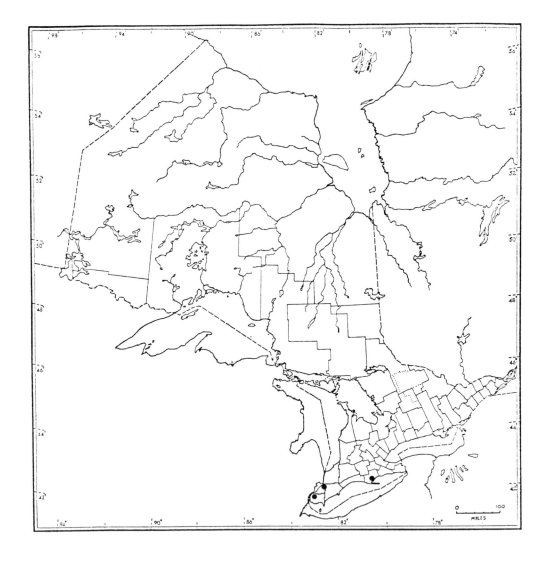

SPECIES: *Erynnis persius* (Scudder)

Persius Dusky Wing

TIMETABLE:

Apr.	May	June	July	Aug.	Sep.	Oct.
Larva----						
	Pupa					
	Adult----					
		Eggs				
		Larva-------------------------------				

Broods   One.

Hibernates   As a mature larva.

OCCURRENCE:

Habitat   Edges of woods with poplars.

Food Plant   Willows, poplars and aspens.

Distribution   Rare in the southern part of the province. However, it seems to be more common in the southern James Bay region.

Status   S3

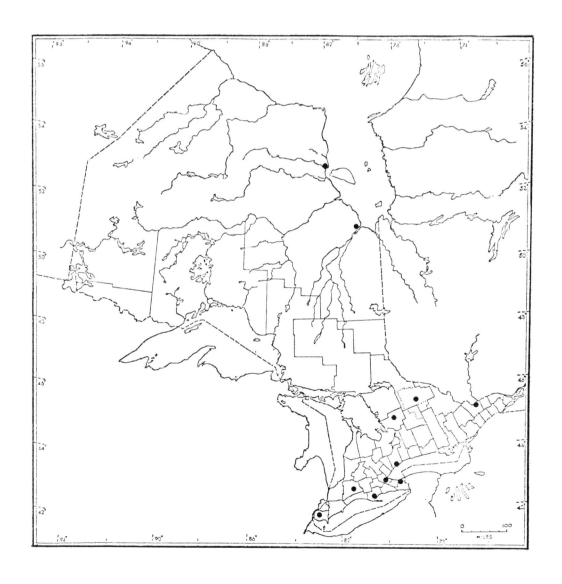

SPECIES: *Pyrgus centaureae* (Rambur)   Grizzled Skipper

TIMETABLE:

Apr.	May	June	July	Aug.	Sep.	Oct.
Pupa------------						
		Adult--				
		Eggs-				
			Larva------------			
					Pupa--------------	

Broods   One, possibly with a two year life cycle.

Hibernates   Not certainly known but probably as a pupa.

OCCURRENCE:

Habitat   Tundra, bogs and open spaces in northern woods.

Food Plant   Cloudberry and wild strawberry.

Distribution   Widespread but primarily a sub-arctic and Canadian Zone species recorded as far south as the vicinity of Lake Superior. A single specimen is reported as having been taken near Ottawa in 1974.

Status   S4

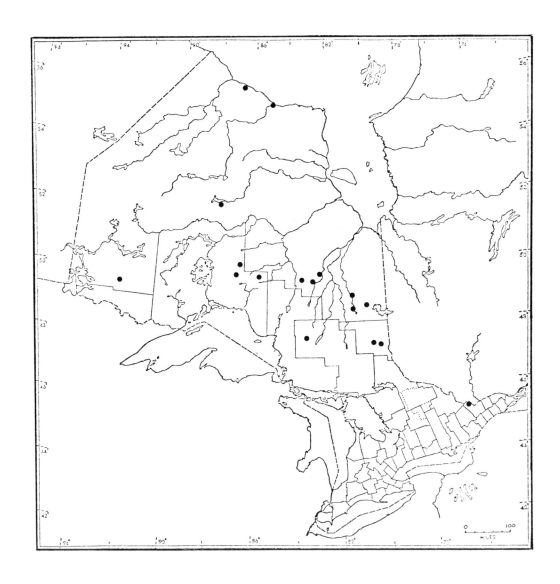

SPECIES: *Pyrgus communis* (Grote)   Checkered Skipper

TIMETABLE:

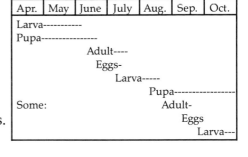

Apr.	May	June	July	Aug.	Sep.	Oct.

Broods   Probably two.

Hibernates   Not certainly known but said to hibernate as
                either larva or pupa.

OCCURRENCE:

Habitat   Fields, open spaces and roadsides in dry areas.

Food Plant   Various mallows.

Distribution   An occasional visitor from the southern States. It has been known to survive here
                for a number of years and a colony existed near St. Catharines for some time during
                the 1950's & 60's. Single specimens were taken in Toronto in 1982 and in Windsor
                in 1988.

Status   S1

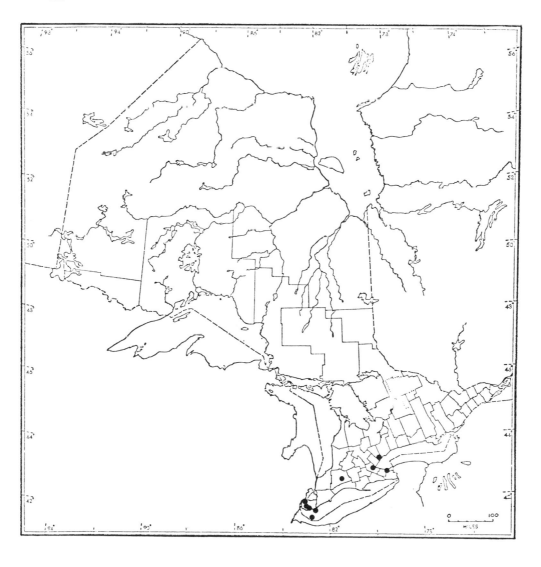

SPECIES: *Pholisora catullus* (Fabricius)　　　　　　　　Common Sooty Wing

TIMETABLE:

Apr.	May	June	July	Aug.	Sep.	Oct.
Larva-------						
	Pupa					
	Adult----------					
	Eggs-----					
	Larva-----					
		Pupa				
		Adult---------				
		Eggs-----				
		Larva-----------------				

Broods　　　　　Two.

Hibernates　　　As a mature larva.

OCCURRENCE:

Habitat　　　　Gardens, disturbed areas, roadsides and the edges of woods.

Food Plant　　Various members of the goosefoot, amaranth and mint families.

Distribution　Widespread but seldom common, most prevalent in the southwestern part of the province but also recorded from the vicinity of Peterborough, Ottawa and Muskoka.

Status　　　　S4

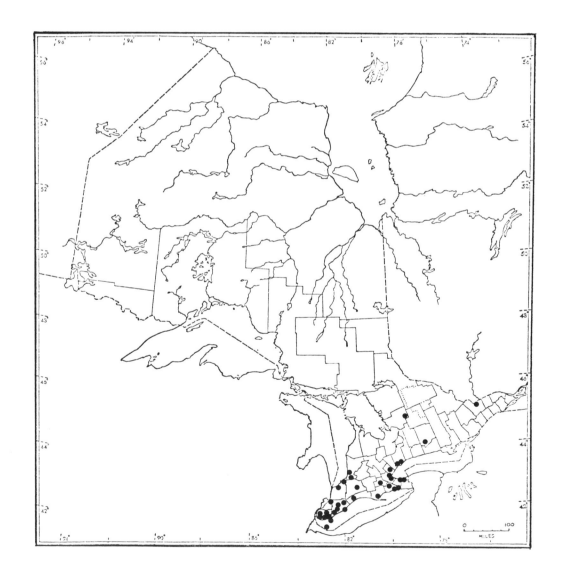

SPECIES: *Carterocephalus palaemon* (Pallas)　　　　　　　　　　　　　　Arctic Skipper

TIMETABLE:

Apr.	May	June	July	Aug.	Sep.	Oct.
Larva--------------						
	Pupa					
		Adult-----				
		Eggs-----				
			Larva-------------------------------			

Broods　　　　　One.

Hibernates　　　As a mature larva.

OCCURRENCE:

Habitat　　　　　Grassy meadows, wetlands and woodland trails.

Food Plant　　　Grasses, preferably broad-leaved varieties.

Distribution　　A typically Canadian Zone species that ranges south to Lake Ontario and north into the Hudson Bay Lowlands. Generally common within this range but becomes more local in the south. Not so far recorded in the extreme southwestern counties.

Status　　　　　S5

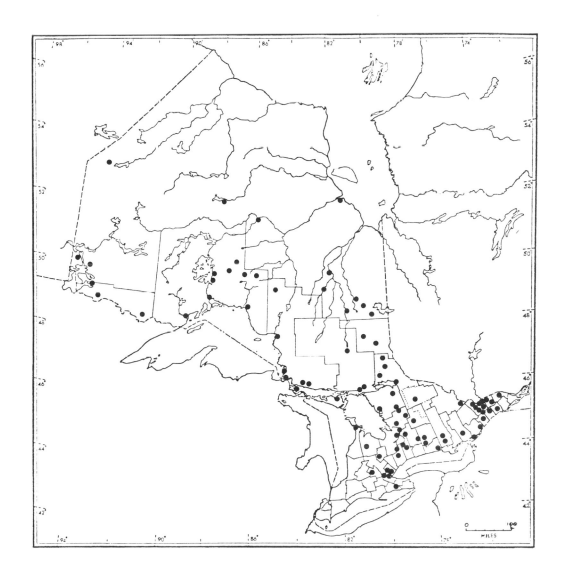

SPECIES: *Ancyloxypha numitor* (Fabricius)

Least Skipper

TIMETABLE:

	Apr.	May	June	July	Aug.	Sep.	Oct.
	Larva-------						
		Pupa					
			Adult--------				
			Eggs------				
				Larva-----------			
					Pupa-------		
					Adult--------		
						Larva-----------------	
	Some:					Pupa	
						Adult	
						Egg	
							Larva-----

Broods   Two, and sometimes three in the south.

Hibernates   As a mature larva.

OCCURRENCE:

Habitat   Grassy & marshy areas, particularly with long grass & reeds.

Food Plant   Various grasses including blue grass, rice cut grass and marsh millet.

Distribution   Common in the southern and central parts of the province and recorded as far north as Lake Abitibi and Lake of the Woods.

Status   S5

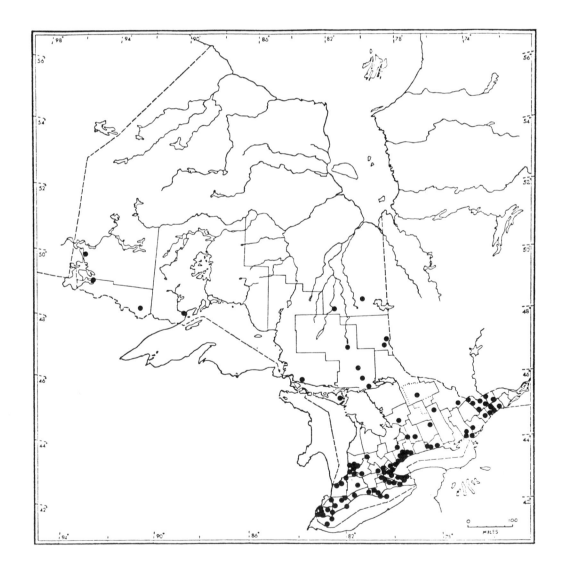

SPECIES: *Oarisma garita* (Reakirt)   Garita Skipper

TIMETABLE:

Apr.	May	June	July	Aug.	Sep.	Oct.
Larva------------						
		Pupa				
		Adult-----				
			Eggs----			
			Larva------------------------			

Broods   One.

Hibernates   As a larva.

OCCURRENCE:

Habitat   Grassy areas and limestone barrens.

Food Plant   Various grasses.

Distribution   Recently discovered in the province in the Great La Cloche Island area of Manitoulin.

Status   S2? (unknown?)

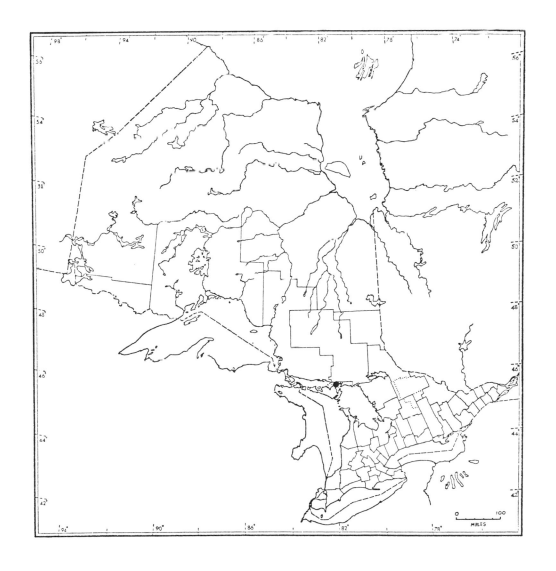

SPECIES: *Thymelicus lineola* (Ochsenheimer)　　　　　European Skipper

TIMETABLES:

Broods　　　One.

Hibernates　　As an egg.

Apr.	May	June	July	Aug.	Sep.	Oct.
Eggs---------						
	Larva--------------					
		Pupa----------				
			Adult------------			
				Eggs--------------------------		

OCCURRENCE:

Habitat　　　Fields, open spaces and roadsides. Particularly where there are flowers.

Food Plant　Timothy, red top and other grasses.

Distribution　Not indigenous. First introduced at London, Ontario in the first decade of this century. From here it has spread over most of the province as far west as Kenora and north to Moosonee. It is now very common and appears still to be spreading.

Status　　　S5

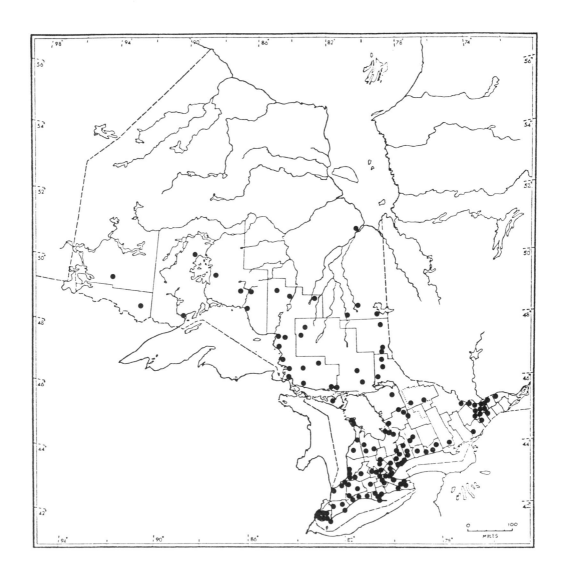

SPECIES: *Hylephila phyleus* (Drury)   Fiery Skipper

TIMETABLE:

Apr.	May	June	July	Aug.	Sep.	Oct.
				Immigrant		
				Adult----------------		
				Eggs--------------		
				Larva----------		
					Pupa---	
					Adult	

Broods   One, and perhaps two in favourable years.

Hibernates   Not resident.

OCCURRENCE:

Habitat   Open spaces and roadsides.

Food Plant   Weedy grasses, especially crabgrass.

Distribution   A rare migrant. A few specimens occasionally reach the extreme south of the province
                in late summer or fall.

Status   SN

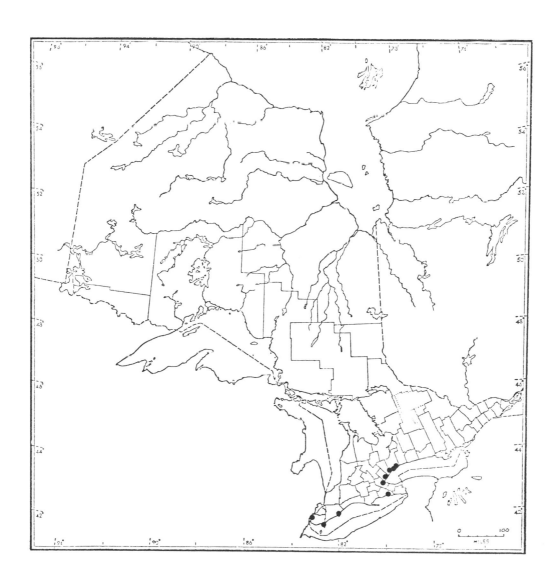

SPECIES: *Hesperia comma* (Linnaeus)

Laurentian Skipper

TIMETABLE:

Apr.	May	June	July	Aug.	Sep.	Oct.
Eggs---------						
	Larva----------					
			Pupa			
			Adult--			
			Eggs---------------------			

Broods   One.

Hibernates   As an egg.

OCCURRENCE:

Habitat   Roadsides and woodland trails.

Food Plant   Perennial bunch grasses, including needlegrass, blue grass, fescue and brome grass.

Distribution Essentially a Canadian Zone species that is widespread from Algonquin Park northwards to the shore of Hudson Bay.

Status   S5

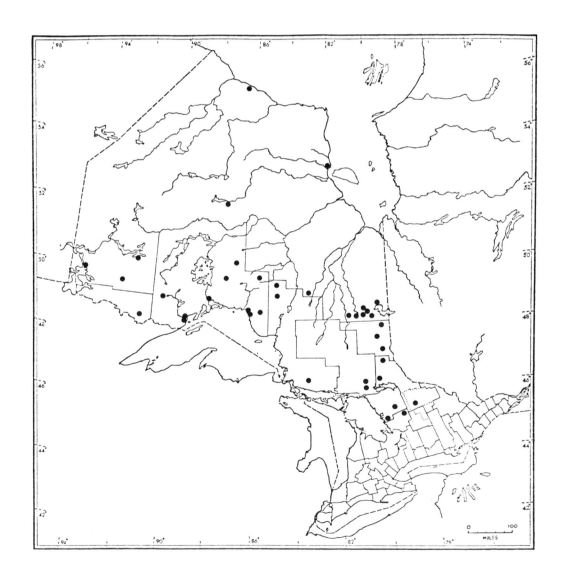

SPECIES: *Hesperia leonardus* Harris

TIMETABLE:

Broods   One.

Hibernates As a young larva.

OCCURRENCE:

Habitat   Fields and woodland trails, especially in sandy areas.

Food Plant   Various grasses, including switch, poverty oat and bent grass.

Distribution Widespread and sometimes locally common in the southern part of the province. Recorded as far north as Algonquin Park and Manitoulin Island. Recent records also from the Thunder Bay area.

Status   S4

Leonardus Skipper

Apr.	May	June	July	Aug.	Sep.	Oct.
Larva------------------------						
			Pupa			
				Adult----		
					Eggs	
						Larva---------

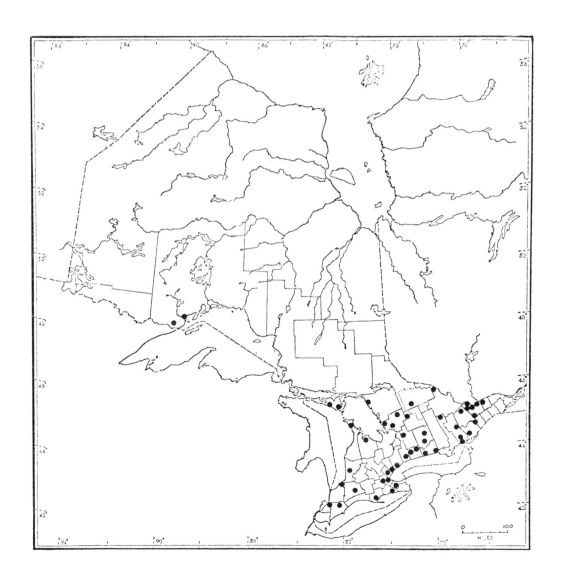

SPECIES: *Hesperia sassacus* Harris

TIMETABLE:

| Broods | One. |
| Hibernates | As a pupa. |

Indian Skipper

Apr.	May	June	July	Aug.	Sep.	Oct.
Pupa--------------						
		Adult-------				
		Eggs---				
			Larva--------			
					Pupa------------	

OCCURRENCE:

Habitat	Meadows and open spaces.
Food Plant	Grasses including panic grass, little bluestem and red fescue.
Distribution	Widespread in the southern and central parts of the province and recorded as far north as Lake of the Woods and the north shore of Lake Superior.
Status	S4

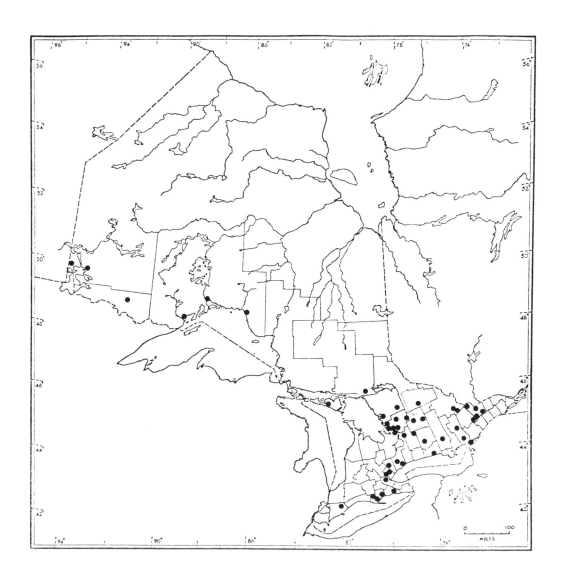

34

SPECIES: *Polites peckius* (W. Kirby)   Peck's Skipper

TIMETABLE:

Broods   Usually one, but there may be a partial second in the south.

Hibernates   As a larva or pupa.

OCCURRENCE:

Habitat   Open grassy fields and roadsides, especially if flowers are present.

Food Plant   Rice grass and probably other grasses.

Distribution Widespread and fairly common throughout the province as far north as the limits of the Canadian Zone..

Status   S5

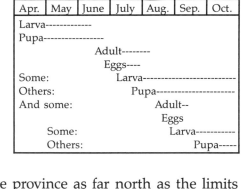

Apr.	May	June	July	Aug.	Sep.	Oct.
Larva-------------						
Pupa----------------						
		Adult--------				
		Eggs----				
Some:			Larva-----------------------			
Others:			Pupa---------------------			
And some:				Adult--		
				Eggs		
Some:				Larva-----------		
Others:					Pupa-----	

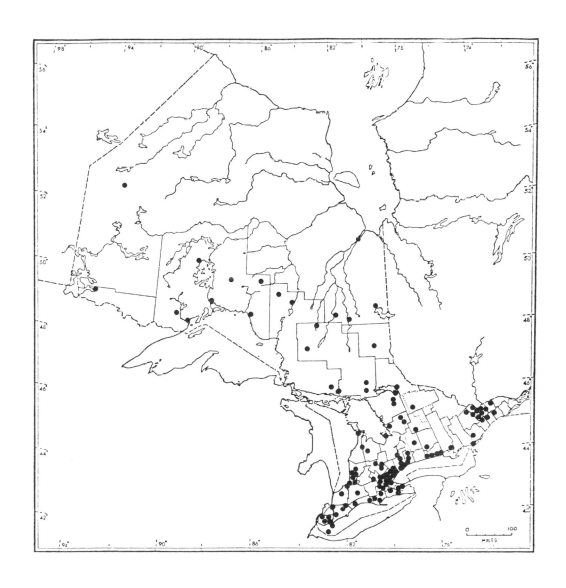

35

SPECIES: *Polites themistocles* (Latreille)   Tawny Edged Skipper

TIMETABLE:

Apr.	May	June	July	Aug.	Sep.	Oct.
Pupa--------------						
	Adult------------					
	Eggs------					
	Larva-------					
			Pupa-------------------			
Some:			Adult			
			Eggs			
			Larva----------			
			Pupa-			

Broods   Usually one, but there may be a partial second in the south.

Hibernates   As a pupa.

OCCURRENCE:

Habitat   Open grassy fields and roadsides.

Food Plant   Panic grasses.

Distribution   Common throughout the province and recorded north to the Albany River.

Status   S5

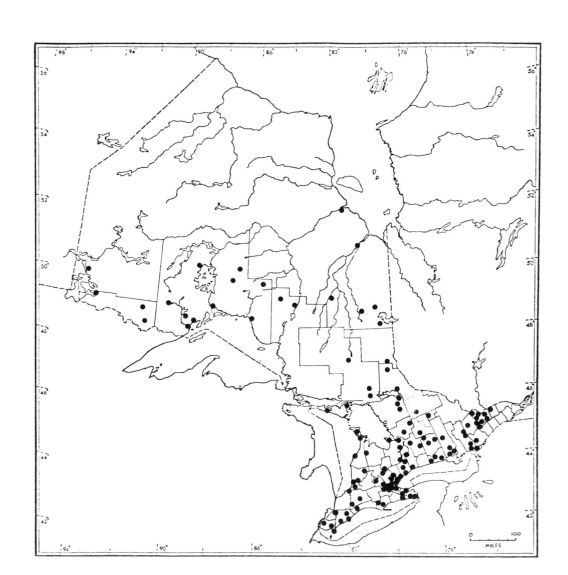

SPECIES: *Polites origenes* (Fabricius)   Cross Line Skipper

Apr.	May	June	July	Aug.	Sep.	Oct.
Larva--------------						
		Pupa				
		Adult-----				
		Eggs-----				
			Larva-----------------------			

TIMETABLE:

Broods   One.

Hibernates   As a mature larva.

OCCURRENCE:

Habitat   Roadsides, fields and hillsides.

Food Plant   Purpletop grass and probably other grasses.

Distribution   Widespread but not common, tending to be rather local over the southern part of the province as far north as Manitoulin, Muskoka and Renfrew.

Status   S4

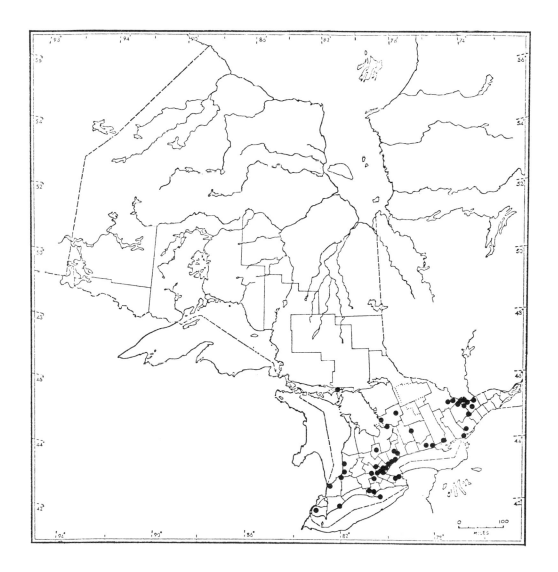

SPECIES: *Polites mystic* (W.H. Edwards) Long Dash

TIMETABLE:

Apr.	May	June	July	Aug.	Sep.	Oct.
Larva-----------						
	Pupa					
		Adult--------				
		Eggs----				
		Larva-------------------------------				
Some:			Pupa			
			Adult			
			Eggs			
			Larva-----------			

Broods   Usually one, but there may be a partial second in the south.

Hibernates   As a mature larva.

OCCURRENCE:

Habitat   Open grassy fields and roadsides, especially with flowers.

Food Plant   Various grasses, especially quack, barnyard, timothy and blue grass.

Distribution   Widespread and frequent throughout the province, recorded as far north as Ekwan Point on the west coast of James Bay.

Status   S5

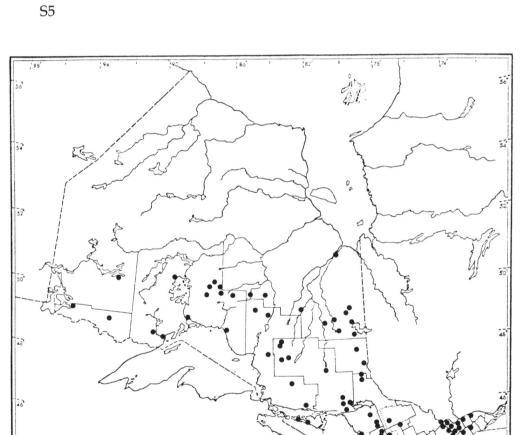

SPECIES: *Wallengrenia egeremet* (Scudder)

TIMETABLE:

Broods   One.

Hibernates As a half grown larva.

OCCURRENCE:

Habitat   Grassy fields and marshy areas.

Food Plant   Not certain, probably panic grasses.

Distribution Widespread and locally common, mainly in the south, but recorded as far north as Lake Abitibi.

Status   S5

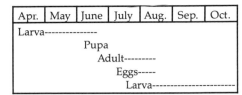

Northern Broken Dash

Apr.	May	June	July	Aug.	Sep.	Oct.
Larva--------------						
		Pupa				
		Adult---------				
			Eggs-----			
				Larva---------------------		

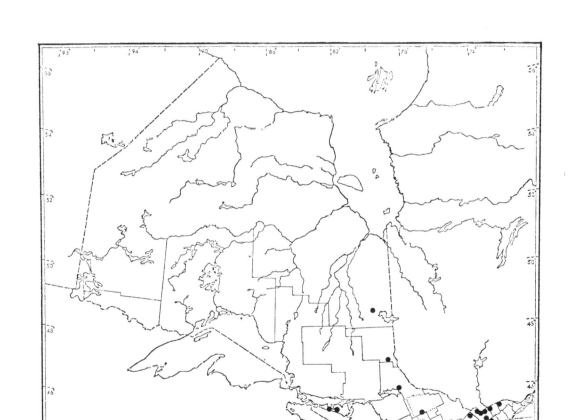

SPECIES: *Pompeius verna* (W.H. Edwards)   Little Glassy Wing

TIMETABLE:

Apr.	May	June	July	Aug.	Sep.	Oct.
Larva--------------						
		Pupa				
		Adult--------				
			Eggs----			
				Larva--------------------		

Broods   One.

Hibernates   Probably as a larva.

OCCURRENCE:

Habitat   Grassy fields and roadsides, particularly with long grass.

Food Plant   Purpletop grass.

Distribution   Local and uncommon, it appears mainly confined to the southwestern part of the province but has also been recorded from Ottawa.

Status   S3

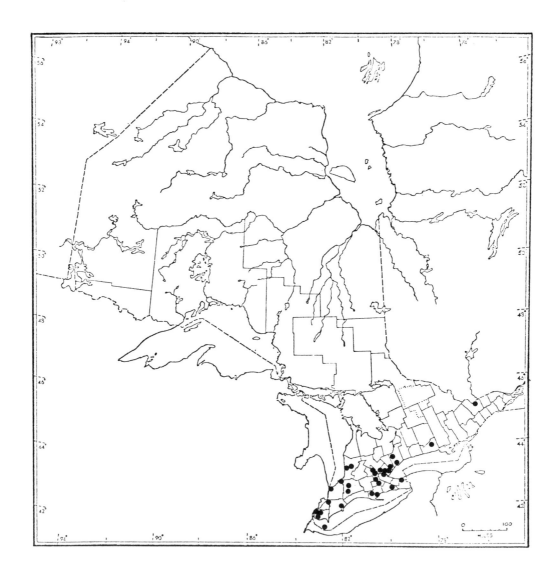

40

SPECIES: *Atrytone logan* (W.H. Edwards)   Delaware Skipper

TIMETABLE:

Apr.	May	June	July	Aug.	Sep.	Oct.

Broods   One.

Larva----------
Pupa--------------------

Hibernates   Apparently as either a larva or pupa.

Adult------
Eggs--

OCCURRENCE:

Some: Larva--------------------
Others: Pupa------

Habitat   Open spaces and woodland trails.

Food Plant   Grasses, including blue stem, switch and woolly beard grass.

Distribution   Widespread but mainly restricted to the Carolinian Zone, also northwards in sandy
                areas along the east coast of Lake Huron.

Status   S4

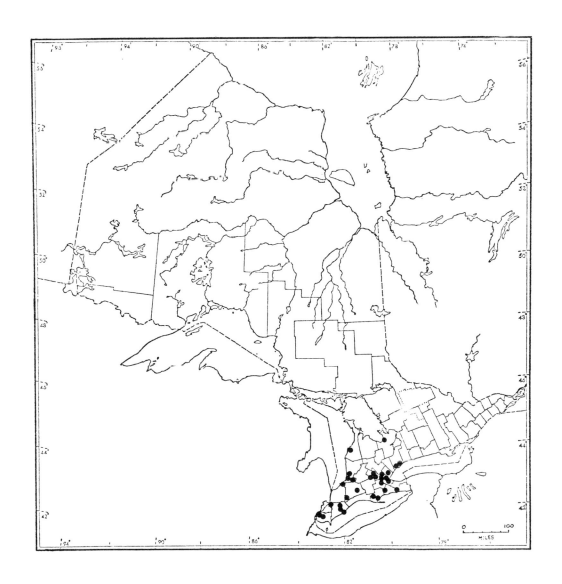

SPECIES: *Poanes massasoit* (Scudder) Mulberry Wing

TIMETABLE

Apr.	May	June	July	Aug.	Sep.	Oct.
Larva------------						
		Pupa				
		Adult-----				
		Eggs----				
			Larva------------------------			

Broods   One.

Hibernates   As a larva.

OCCURRENCE

Habitat   Marshy or wet areas with long grass and sedges.

Food Plant   Sedge, especially *Carex stricta*.

Distribution Very local and found in widely scattered colonies in the southern parts of the province.

Status   S3

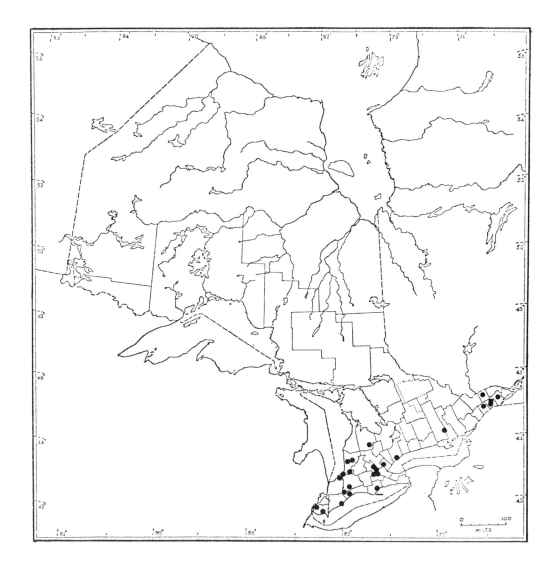

SPECIES: *Poanes hobomok* (Harris)   Hobomok Skipper

TIMETABLE

Apr.	May	June	July	Aug.	Sep.	Oct.
Pupa--------------						
	Adult--------					
		Eggs				
		Larva------------------				
				Pupa--------------		

Broods   One.

Hibernates   Probably as a pupa.

OCCURRENCE

Habitat   Fields, open spaces, roadsides and woodland trails.

Food Plant   Grasses, including panic grasses and blue grass.

Distribution   Widespread and frequent throughout most of the province as far north as Lake
               Attawapiskat. The female form *pocahontas* has been recorded as far north as
               Timiskaming.

Status   S5

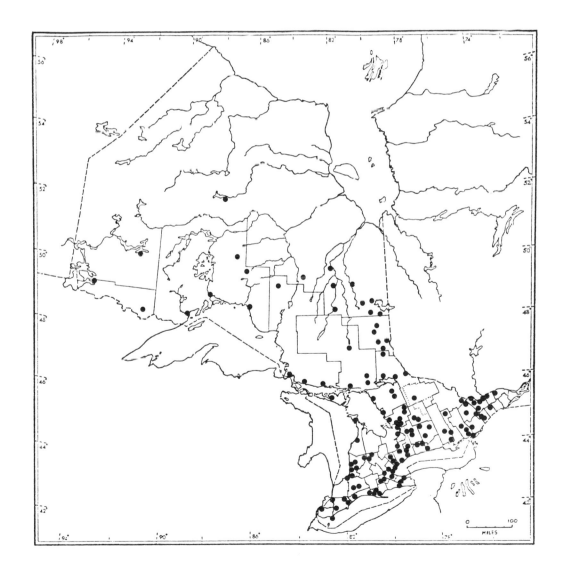

SPECIES: *Poanes viator* (W.H. Edwards)   Broad Winged Skipper

TIMETABLE

Apr.	May	June	July	Aug.	Sep.	Oct.
Larva----------						
		Pupa				
		Adult------				
		Eggs------				
			Larva----------------------			

Broods   One.

Hibernates   Probably as a larva.

OCCURRENCE

Habitat   Marshy and wet areas with long grass and sedges.

Food Plant   Sedges and some grasses including wild rice and panic grasses.

Distribution   A mainly Carolinian species locally common in wetlands in the south and east of the province.

Status   S4

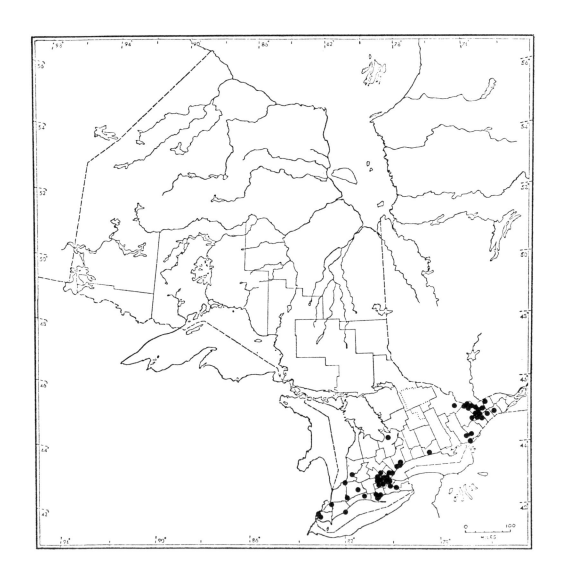

44

SPECIES: *Euphyes dion* (W.H. Edwards)   Dion Skipper

TIMETABLE

Apr.	May	June	July	Aug.	Sep.	Oct.
Larva--------------						
		Pupa				
		Adult------				
			Eggs---			
				Larva----------------------		

Broods   One.

Hibernates   As a half grown larva.

OCCURRENCE

Habitat   Marshy areas and damp meadows, especially those with long grass and sedges.

Food Plant   Sedges.

Distribution Widespread but local in marshes in the south and east of the province.

Status   S4

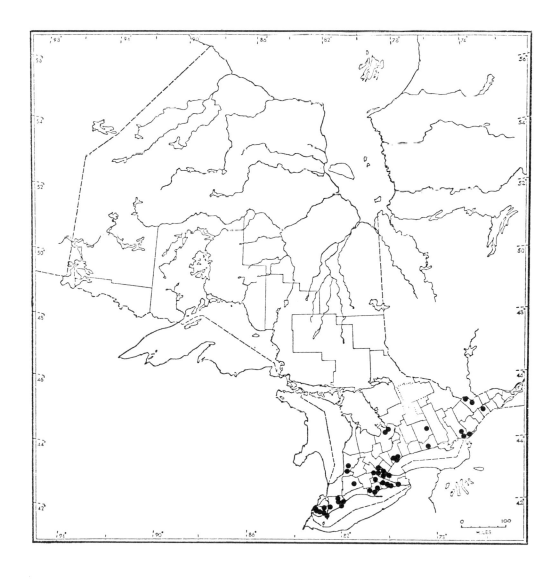

SPECIES: *Euphyes dukesi* (Lindsey)   Duke's Skipper

TIMETABLE

Apr.	May	June	July	Aug.	Sep.	Oct.
Larva--------------------						
		Pupa				
			Adult---			
			Eggs			
			Larva--------------------			

Broods   One.

Hibernates   Probably as a larva.

OCCURRENCE

Habitat   Marshy areas, roadsides and woods with long grass and sedges.

Food Plant   Sedges.

Distribution   Discovered in the province on July 11th, 1968 by A.M. Holmes; so far only recorded in the extreme southwest.

Status   S3

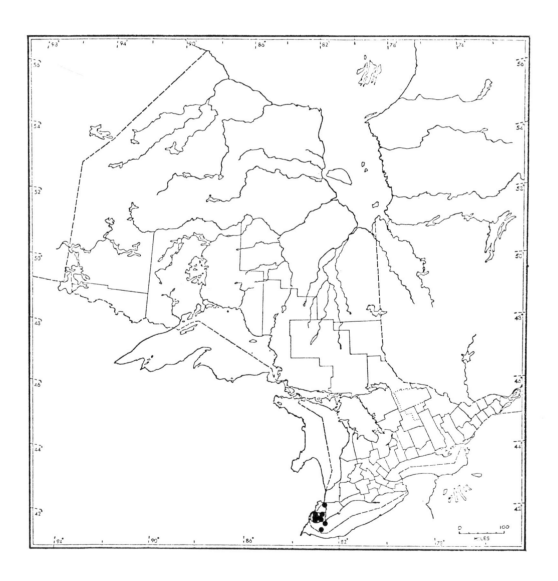

SPECIES: *Euphyes conspicua* (W.H. Edwards)   Black Dash

TIMETABLE

Apr.	May	June	July	Aug.	Sep.	Oct.
Larva------------						
		Pupa				
		Adult-----------				
			Eggs---------			
				Larva-----------------------		

Broods   One.

Hibernates   Probably as a larva.

OCCURRENCE

Habitat   Marshy or wet areas, especially those with long grass and sedges.

Food Plant   Sedges.

Distribution   In widely scattered and local colonies in the Carolinian Zone.

Status   S4

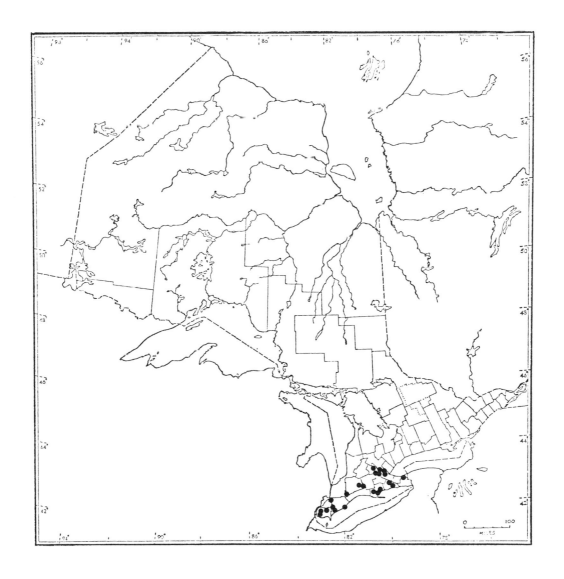

47

SPECIES: *Euphyes bimacula* (Grote & Robinson)　　　　　　Two Spotted Skipper

TIMETABLE

Apr.	May	June	July	Aug.	Sep.	Oct.
Larva------------						
		Pupa				
		Adult--				
		Eggs				
			Larva------------------------			

Broods　　　　　One.

Hibernates　　　As a half grown larva.

OCCURRENCE

Habitat　　　　　Marshy areas and damp meadows.

Food Plant　　　Sedges.

Distribution　　Very local, in marshes in the southern part of the province, north to Manitoulin Island, Sudbury and Lake Nipissing.

Status　　　　　S3

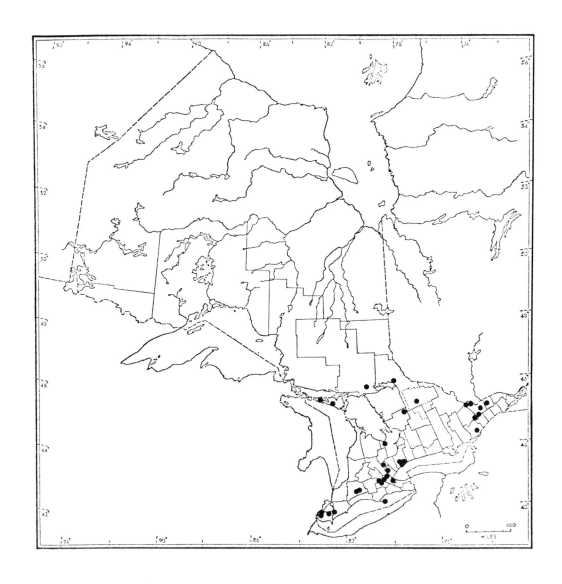

48

SPECIES: *Euphyes vestris* (Boisduval)   Dun Skipper

TIMETABLE

Broods   Usually one, but there may be a partial second
              in the south.

Hibernates   As a half grown larva.

OCCURRENCE

Habitat   Open fields and roadsides, especially where
              there are long grasses and flowers.

Food Plant   Sedges.

Distribution Widespread and frequent as far north as Lake Abitibi, Lake Nipigon and Lake of the
              Woods.

Status   S5

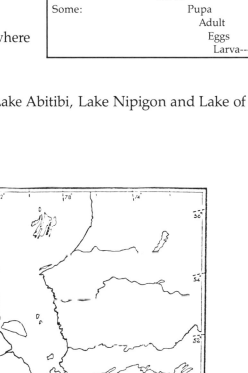

Apr.	May	June	July	Aug.	Sep.	Oct.
Larva-------------						
		Pupa------				
		Adult---------				
			Eggs-----			
			Larva----------------------			
Some:				Pupa		
				Adult		
				Eggs		
					Larva-------	

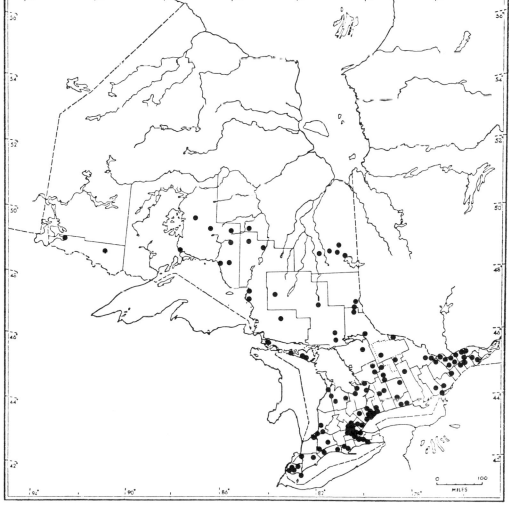

49

SPECIES: *Atrytonopsis hianna* (Scudder)   Dusted Skipper

TIMETABLE

Apr.	May	June	July	Aug.	Sep.	Oct.
Larva-----						
	Pupa					
	Adult					
		Eggs				
		Larva--------------------------------				

Broods   One.

Hibernates   As a mature larva.

OCCURRENCE

Habitat   Dry sand hills.

Food Plant   Big and little bluestem grasses.

Distribution Known only from the Pinery and Ipperwash areas of Lambton County, where it is very local.

Status   S2

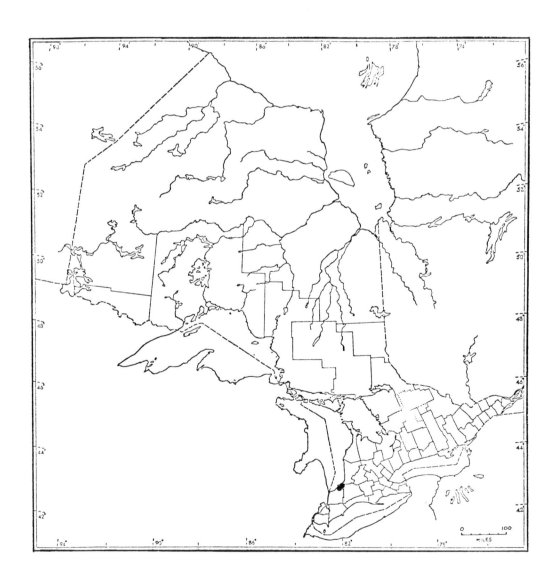

SPECIES: *Amblyscirtes hegon* (Scudder)

Pepper and Salt Skipper

TIMETABLE

Apr.	May	June	July	Aug.	Sep.	Oct.
Larva------						
	Pupa					
	Adult------					
		Eggs				
		Larva--------------------------------				

Broods   One.

Hibernates   As a larva.

OCCURRENCE

Habitat   Roadsides and trails, especially in forests.

Food Plant   Grasses including blue and indian grass.

Distribution   Rare and not well known, recorded mainly in the southerly parts of the Canadian
               Zone, also recently from the Lake of the Woods area and St. Williams.

Status   S3

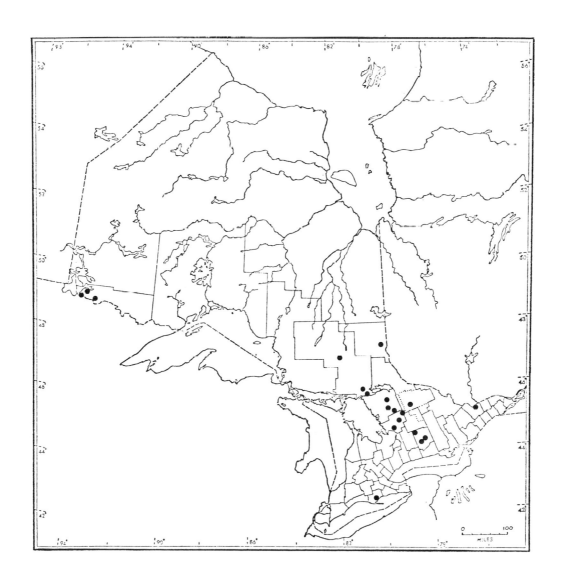

51

SPECIES: *Amblyscirtes vialis* (W.H. Edwards)   Roadside Skipper

TIMETABLE

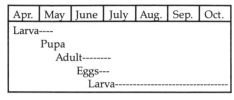

Apr.	May	June	July	Aug.	Sep.	Oct.
Larva----						
	Pupa					
		Adult-------				
			Eggs---			
			Larva-----------------------------			

Broods   One.

Hibernates   As a larva.

OCCURRENCE

Habitat   Roadsides, trails and open spaces, especially in forests.

Food Plant   Grasses, including blue grass, bent grass and wild oats.

Distribution   Widespread throughout most of the province as far north as Lake Attawapiskat.

Status   S5

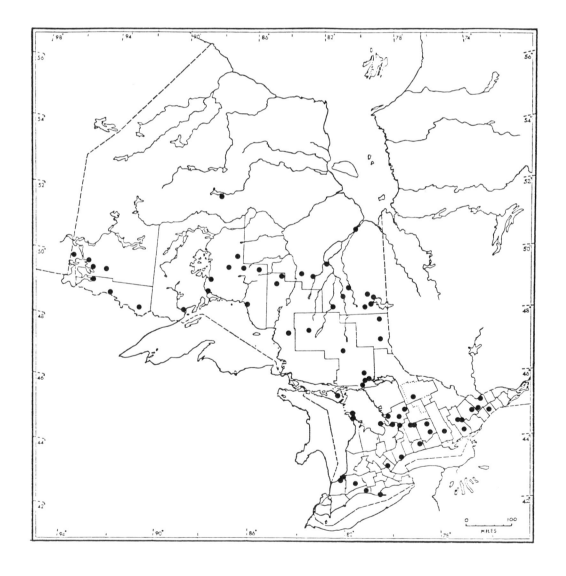

Family: PAPILIONIDAE

The Swallowtail Butterflies

The Giant Swallowtail (*Heraclides cresphontes*) at Point Pelee in 1971.

The Old World Swallowtail (*Papilio machaon*) near Geraldton, June 22, 1971.

Larva of the Black Swallowtail (*Papilio polyxenes*).

SPECIES: *Battus philenor* (Linnaeus)

TIMETABLE:

Broods   Two, and occasionally a partial third.

Hibernates   Not known to hibernate in Ontario, but there is some evidence it may occasionally be resident for several years. If so, it would presumably hibernate as a pupa.

OCCURRENCE:

Habitat   Fields and open spaces, especially where there are flowers.

Food Plant   Pipe vine.

Distribution A rare immigrant recorded occasionally from southwestern Ontario and the shore of Lake Ontario. A stray was once recorded from Caribou Island, Lake Superior.

Status   S2

Pipe Vine Swallowtail

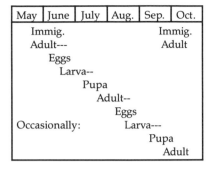

May	June	July	Aug.	Sep.	Oct.
Immig.					Immig.
Adult---					Adult
Eggs					
Larva--					
	Pupa				
	Adult--				
	Eggs				
Occasionally:		Larva---			
		Pupa			
		Adult			

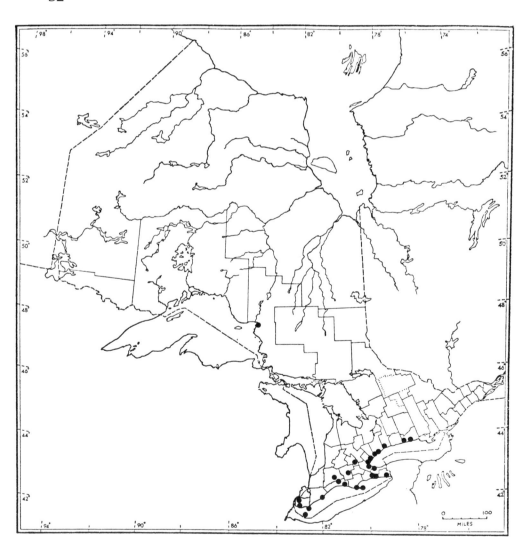

SPECIES: *Papilio polyxenes* Fabricius

Black Swallowtail

TIMETABLE:

Broods   Two, and sometimes three in the south.

Hibernates   As a pupa.

OCCURRENCE:

Habitat   Fields, open woods and open spaces where there are flowers.

Food Plant   Various members of the parsley family.

Distribution Southern Ontario mainly south of the Shield. Isolated records also from Lake of the Woods and the north shore of Lake Superior.

Status   S5

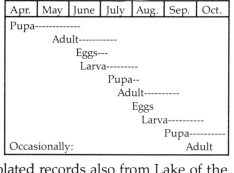

Apr.	May	June	July	Aug.	Sep.	Oct.
Pupa------------						
	Adult-----------					
		Eggs---				
		Larva---------				
			Pupa--			
			Adult----------			
				Eggs		
				Larva----------		
					Pupa----------	
Occasionally:						Adult

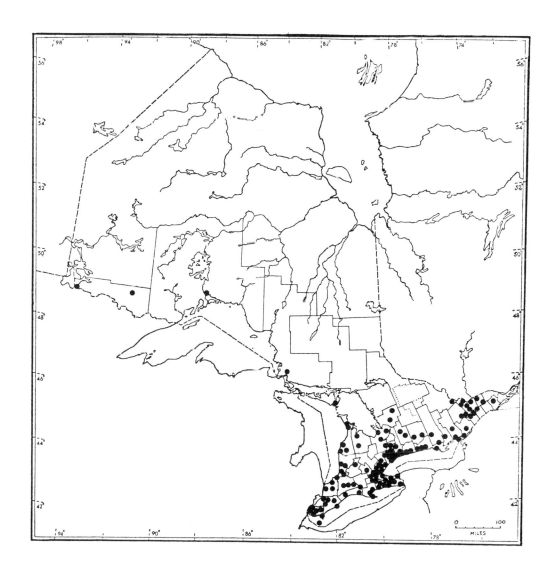

SPECIES: *Papilio machaon* Linnaeus   Old World Swallowtail

TIMETABLE:

Apr.	May	June	July	Aug.	Sep.	Oct.
Pupa-------------						
		Adult-------				
		Eggs				
		Larva-------				
				Pupa---------------------		

Broods   One.

Hibernates   As a pupa.

OCCURRENCE:

Habitat   Open spaces in northwestern forests, especially near sandy jackpine areas.

Food Plant   Scotch Lovage *(Ligusticum scothium)* and probably *Petasites*.

Distribution Uncommon and recorded only from scattered locations between Lake of the Woods, Lake Superior and James Bay.

Status   S4

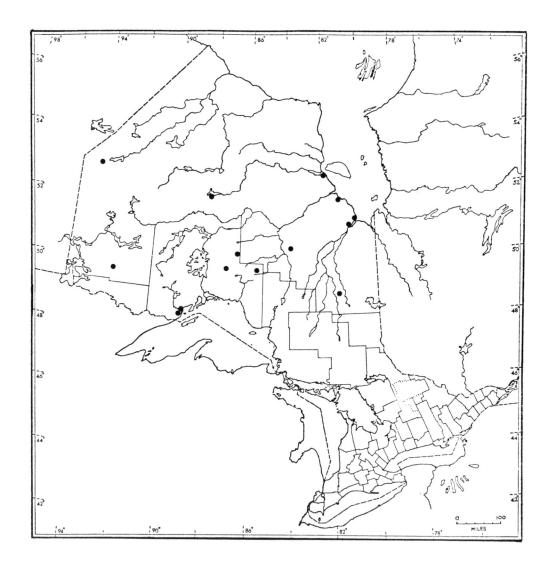

SPECIES: *Heraclides cresphontes* (Cramer)   Giant Swallowtail

TIMETABLE:

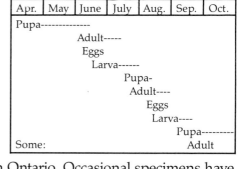

Apr.	May	June	July	Aug.	Sep.	Oct.
Pupa--------------						
	Adult-----					
	Eggs					
		Larva------				
			Pupa-			
			Adult----			
				Eggs		
				Larva----		
					Pupa--------	
Some:						Adult

Broods   Two, and sometimes a partial third.

Hibernates   As a pupa.

OCCURRENCE:

Habitat   Fields, open woods and open spaces, especially where there are flowers.

Food Plant   Prickly ash and hop tree.

Distribution Uncommon and mainly confined to southwestern Ontario. Occasional specimens have been recorded north and east of its normal range.

Status   S3

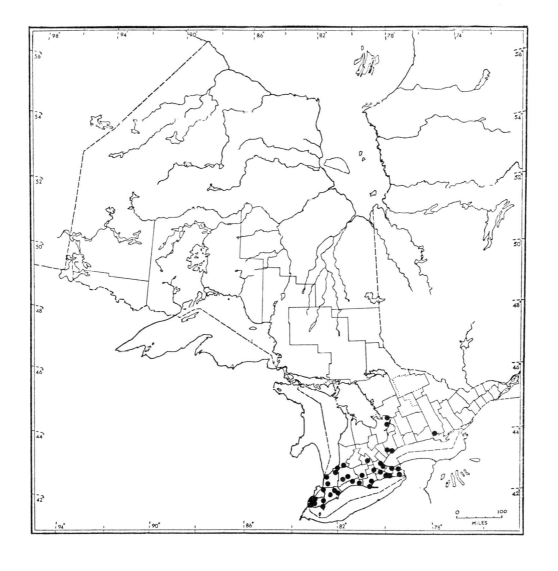

57

SPECIES: *Pterourus glaucus* (Linnaeus)

Tiger Swallowtail

TIMETABLE:

Broods — Two in the south and one in the north.

Hibernates — As a pupa.

OCCURRENCE:

Habitat — Woodlands and open spaces nearby, however it ranges over almost any habitat and may be seen even in large urban areas.

Food Plant — A wide variety of trees and shrubs including birch, poplar, cherry, ash, maple, etc.

Distribution — Widespread and often common over southern and central Ontario north to Hudson Bay. Black female morphs are occasionally seen in southwestern areas.

Status — S5

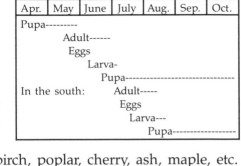

Apr.	May	June	July	Aug.	Sep.	Oct.
Pupa---------						
	Adult------					
	Eggs					
		Larva-				
			Pupa--------------------------------			
In the south:		Adult-----				
		Eggs				
			Larva---			
				Pupa-----------------		

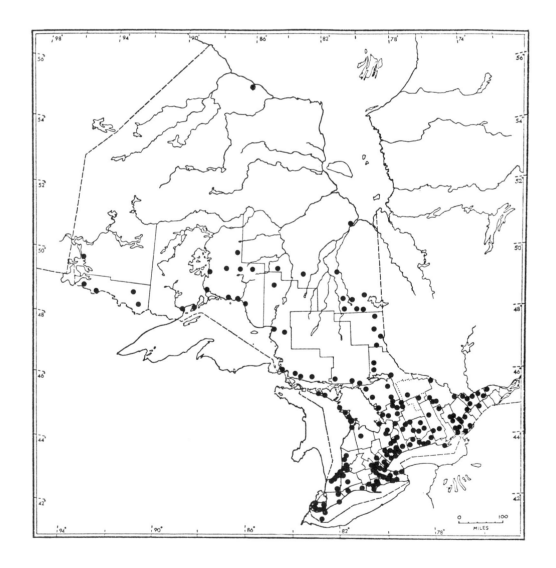

58

SPECIES: *Pterourus troilus* (Linnaeus)

Spicebush Swallowtail

TIMETABLE:

Broods   Two.

Hibernates   As a pupa.

 OCCURRENCE:

Habitat   Fields, open spaces and the edges of woods.

Food Plant   Sassafras, tulip tree and spicebush.

Distribution   Widespread in the Carolinian Zone, over southwestern Ontario and occasionally recorded as far north as Toronto.

Status   S4

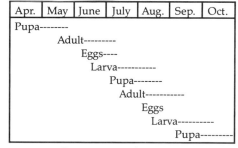

Apr.	May	June	July	Aug.	Sep.	Oct.
Pupa--------						
	Adult---------					
		Eggs----				
		Larva-----------				
			Pupa--------			
			Adult-----------			
				Eggs		
				Larva----------		
					Pupa---------	

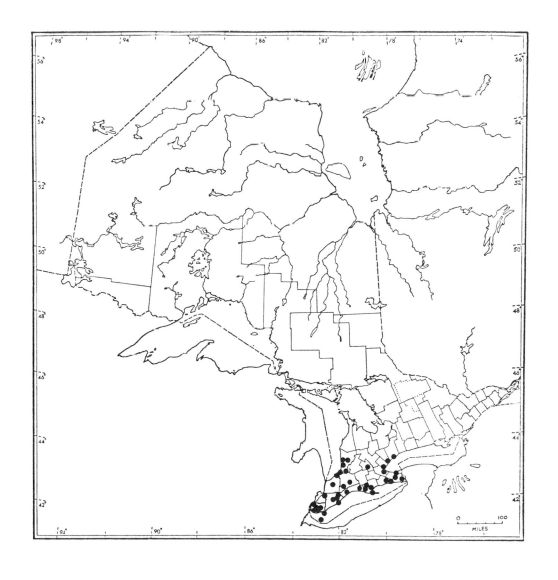

59

The Tiger Swallowtail (*Pterourus glaucus*) at Aurora in 1980.

The Spicebush Swallowtail (*Pterourus troilus*) ex. larva
from St. Williams (Norfolk Co.) female in 1969.

Family: PIERIDAE

The White & Yellow Butterflies

Larva, pupa and adult Olympia Marblewing (*Euchloe olympia*) from Pinery south of Grand Bend (Lambton Co.) in 1975.

SPECIES: *Pontia protodice* (Boisduval & Leconte)

Checkered White

TIMETABLE:

Apr.	May	June	July	Aug.	Sep.	Oct.

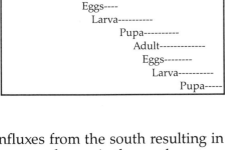

Broods   Two.

Hibernates   As a pupa.

OCCURRENCE:

Habitat   Fields and open spaces.

Food Plant   Various members of the mustard family, including wild peppergrasses, shepherd's purse and winter cress.

Distribution Not a permanent resident. There are occasional influxes from the south resulting in the establishment of transient colonies surviving for several years in the southwestern parts of the province. It also strays northwards as far as Sault Ste. Marie and the lower Ottawa River, where it does not appear to establish itself.

Status   S2

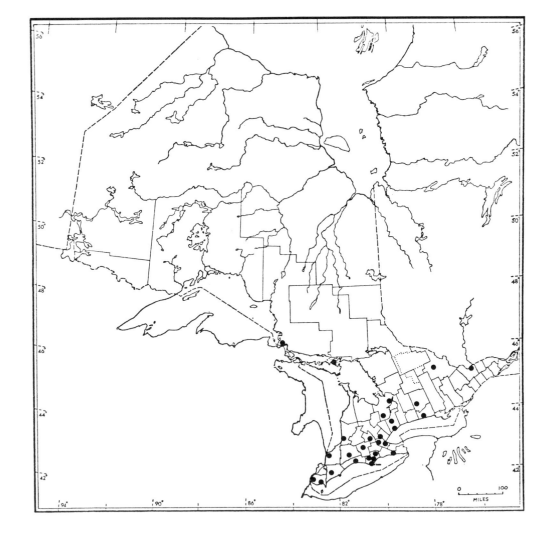

SPECIES: *Pontia occidentalis* (Reakirt)

Western Checkered White

TIMETABLE:

Broods   Two.

Hibernates   As a pupa.

OCCURRENCE:

Habitat   Fields, open spaces and clearings in woods.

Food Plant   Various members of the mustard family.

Distribution   Northwestern Ontario to Hudson Bay, east to Moosonee and as far south as Manitoulin Island.

Status   S3

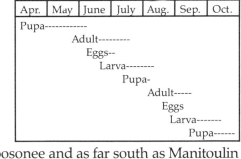

Apr.	May	June	July	Aug.	Sep.	Oct.
Pupa-----------						
	Adult---------					
	Eggs--					
	Larva--------					
		Pupa-				
		Adult-----				
		Eggs				
		Larva-------				
		Pupa------				

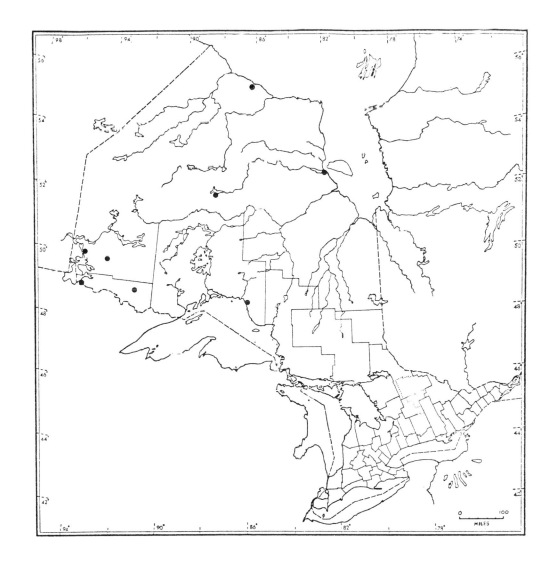

SPECIES: *Pieris napi* (Linnaeus)   Mustard White

TIMETABLE:

Apr.	May	June	July	Aug.	Sep.	Oct.
Pupa--------						
	Adult-----					
	Eggs--					
		Larva---				
		Pupa----				
			Adult-----			
			Eggs			
			Larva------			
				Pupa-----------------		

Broods   Two, sometimes three and a partial fourth.

Hibernates   As a pupa.

OCCURRENCE:

Habitat   Woods, woodland trails and nearby open spaces.

Food Plant   Mustard family including toothworts, various cresses etc..

Distribution   Widespread and sometimes locally common as far north as Hudson Bay.

Status   S5

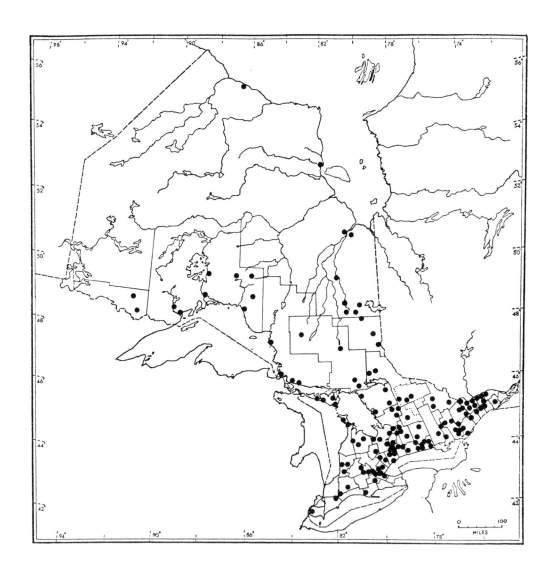

SPECIES: *Pieris virginiensis* (W.H. Edwards)   West Virginia White

TIMETABLE:

Apr.	May	June	July	Aug.	Sep.	Oct.
Pupa------						
Adult--						
Eggs						
Larva-----						
		Pupa-------------------------------				

Broods   One.

Hibernates   As a pupa.

OCCURRENCE:

Habitat   Open woods and woodland trails.

Food Plant   Toothworts, particularly *D. diphylla*.

Distribution   This species is an early spring flier which occurs in some Transition Zone localities. The largest populations live in Halton County and sparser populations exist in nearby counties including Peel, Grey, Waterloo, Middlesex, Lambton and Elgin. Other relatively sparse populations have been recorded in the Algoma District, including St. Joseph and Manitoulin Islands, Frontenac and Lanark Counties. There is an introduced colony in Victoria County. There is a historical record from Simcoe County. The species was protected under The Endangered Species Act, RSO, for a period ending in June, 1990.

Status   S3

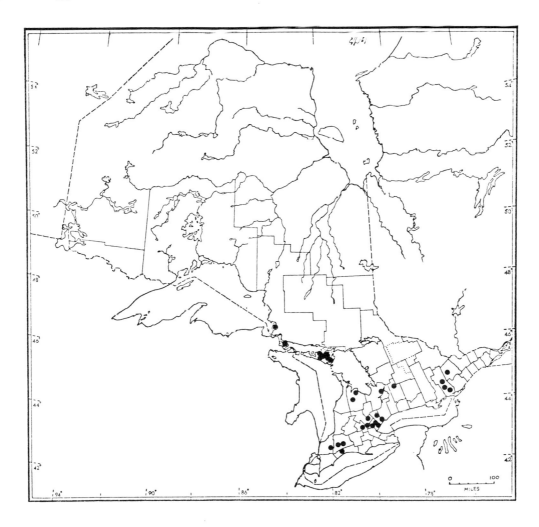

SPECIES: *Pieris rapae* (Linnaeus)   Cabbage White

TIMETABLE:

Apr.	May	June	July	Aug.	Sep.	Oct.
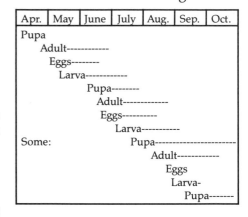

Broods   Two, and sometimes three in the south.

Hibernates   As a pupa.

OCCURRENCE:

Habitat   Almost all open areas, penetrating everywhere except deep woods. Also prevalent in urban areas.

Food Plant   Mustard family, especially domestic varieties, cabbage, etc.

Distribution Common over most of Ontario as far north as Lake of the Woods, Lake Nipigon and James Bay.

Status   S5

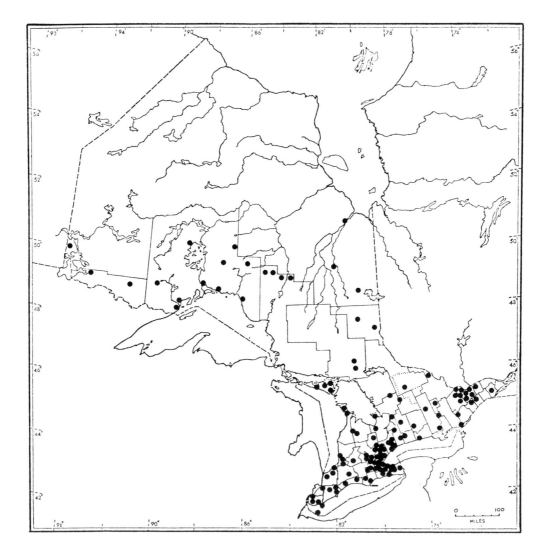

SPECIES: *Euchloe ausonides* Lucas

TIMETABLE:

Broods   One.

Hibernates   As a pupa.

OCCURRENCE:

Habitat   Open areas and roadsides.

Food Plant   Rock cress.

Distribution   Widespread in local colonies in northwestern Ontario west from the Ontario Northland Railway in the Cochrane District and also on Manitoulin Island.

Status   S4

Large Marblewing

Apr.	May	June	July	Aug.	Sep.	Oct.
Pupa---------						
	Adult---------					
		Eggs				
		Larva----				
			Pupa-------------------------			

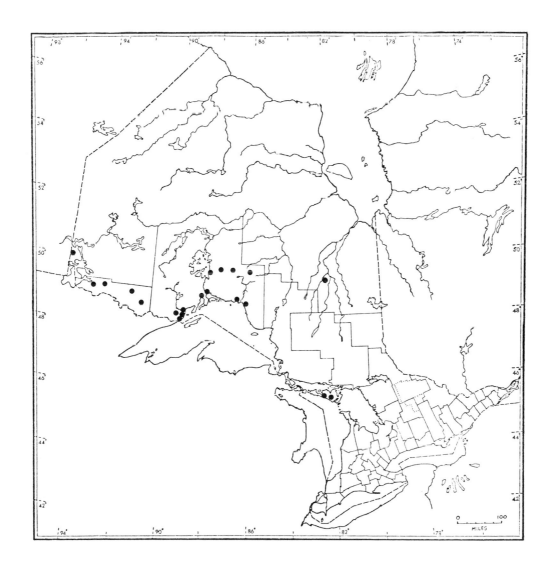

SPECIES: *Euchloe olympia* (W.H. Edwards)　　　　　Olympia Marblewing

TIMETABLE:

Broods　　　One.

Hibernates　　As a pupa.

Apr.	May	June	July	Aug.	Sep.	Oct.
Pupa-------						
	Adult--					
	Eggs					
	Larva----------					
			Pupa--------------------------			

OCCURRENCE:

Habitat　　　Dry open areas in or near woodlands.

Food Plant　　Rock cress and other plants of the Mustard family.

Distribution　Locally common and associated with dry limestone or sandy areas generally between Lake Huron and eastern Ontario.

Status　　　S4

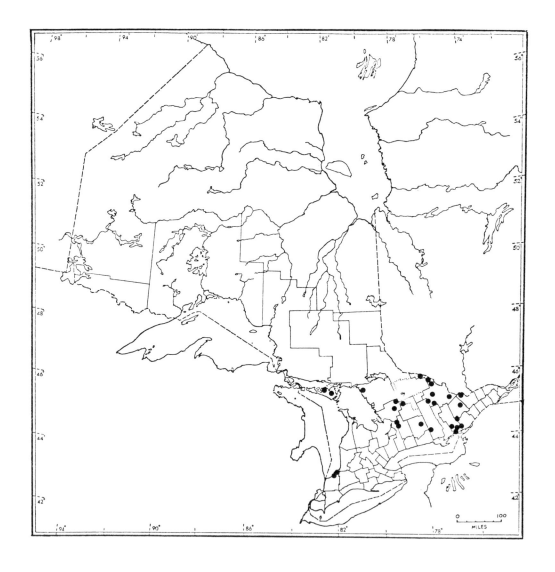

SPECIES: *Colias philodice* Godart

Common Sulphur

TIMETABLE:

| Broods | Two, and sometimes three in the south. |
| Hibernates | As a pupa. |

OCCURRENCE:

Habitat	Fields and roadsides, especially where there are flowers.
Food Plant	White clover, sometimes alfalfa, vetch and locoweed.
Distribution	Common over most of Ontario and recorded as far north as the Albany River.
Status	S5

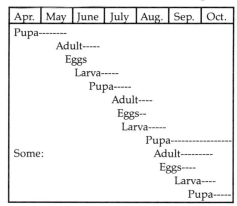

Apr.	May	June	July	Aug.	Sep.	Oct.
Pupa--------						
	Adult-----					
	Eggs					
	Larva-----					
		Pupa-----				
		Adult----				
		Eggs--				
		Larva-----				
			Pupa----------------			
Some:			Adult---------			
			Eggs----			
			Larva----			
			Pupa-----			

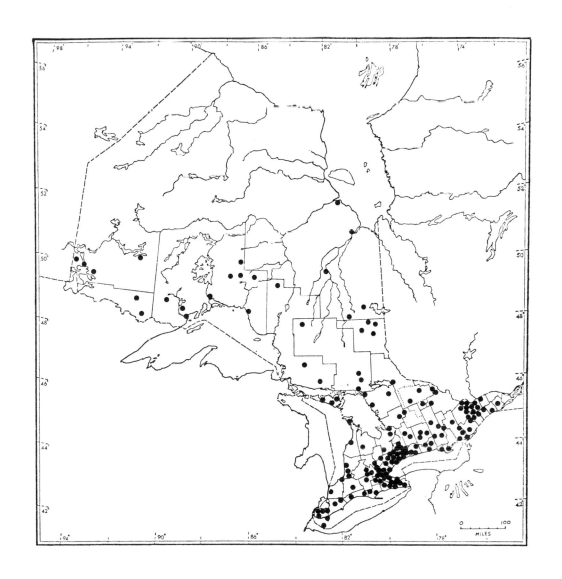

69

SPECIES: *Colias eurytheme* Boisduval

Orange Sulphur

TIMETABLE:

Apr.	May	June	July	Aug.	Sep.	Oct.
Pupa--------------						
		Adult-----------				
		Eggs-----				
		Larva----------				
			Pupa--------			
				Adult-------------		
				Eggs------		
					Larva----------	
						Pupa-------

Broods   Two.

Hibernates   As a pupa.

OCCURRENCE:

Habitat   Fields and roadsides, especially where there are flowers.

Food Plant   Alfalfa, sometimes white clover and locoweed.

Distribution   Common over most of Ontario and recorded as far north as Favourable Lake, Lake Attawapiskat and James Bay.

Status   S5

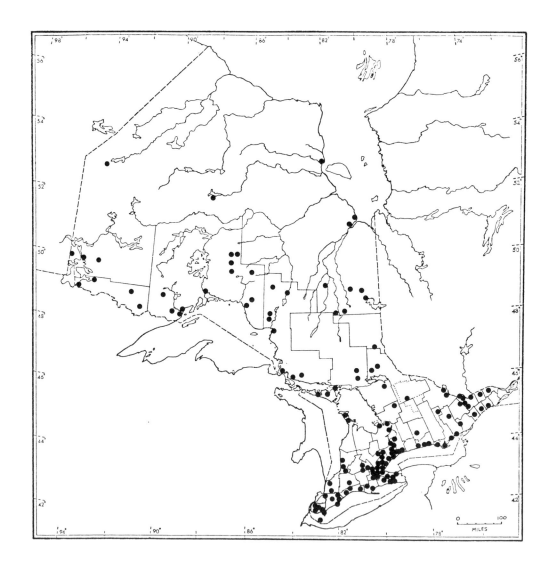

SPECIES: *Colias gigantea* Strecker

TIMETABLE:

Broods   One.

Hibernates   As a half grown larva.

OCCURRENCE:

Habitat   Muskeg, tundra and rough open ground.

Food Plant   Dwarf or snow willow.

Distribution   Recorded only from the shores of Hudson and James Bays.

Status   S3

Giant Sulphur

Apr.	May	June	July	Aug.	Sep.	Oct.
Larva---------------------						
			Pupa			
			Adult			
			Eggs			
				Larva----------------		

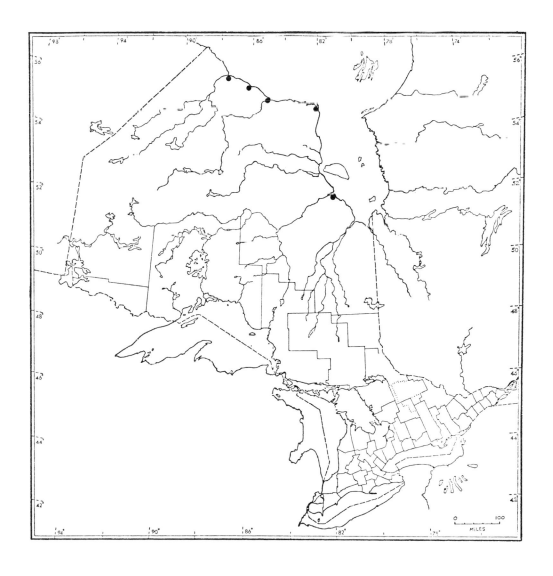

71

SPECIES: *Colias pelidne* Boisduval & Leconte

TIMETABLE:

Broods   One.

Hibernates   As a half grown larva.

OCCURRENCE:

Habitat   Muskeg, tundra and rough open ground.

Food Plant   Uncertain, probably blueberry.

Distribution   Recorded only from Moosonee and the shores of Hudson and James Bays.

Status   S4

Pelidne Sulphur

Apr.	May	June	July	Aug.	Sep.	Oct.
Larva----------------------						
			Pupa			
			Adult			
			Eggs			
				Larva----------------		

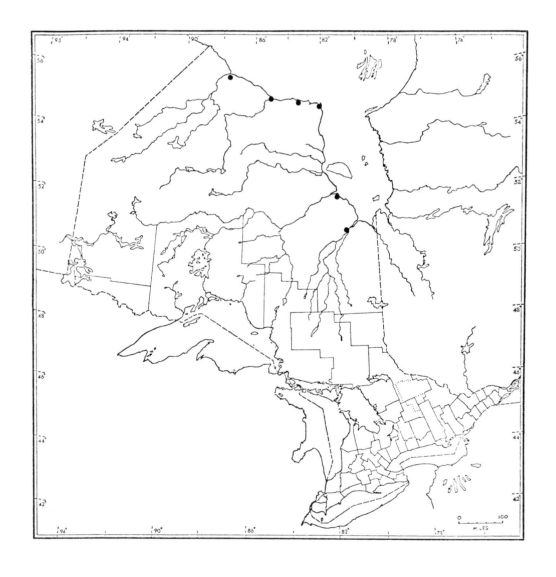

SPECIES: *Colias interior* Scudder

Pink Edged Sulphur

TIMETABLE:

Apr.	May	June	July	Aug.	Sep.	Oct.
Larva--------------						
		Pupa---				
		Adult----------				
			Eggs-----			
			Larva---------------------			

Broods   One.

Hibernates   As a half grown larva.

OCCURRENCE:

Habitat   Acid bogs and jackpine areas in the southerly parts of its range; more widespread in the north in woods and open spaces.

Food Plant   Blueberry.

Distribution   Locally common in its habitat in the south - more generally distributed as far north as Moosonee.

Status   S5

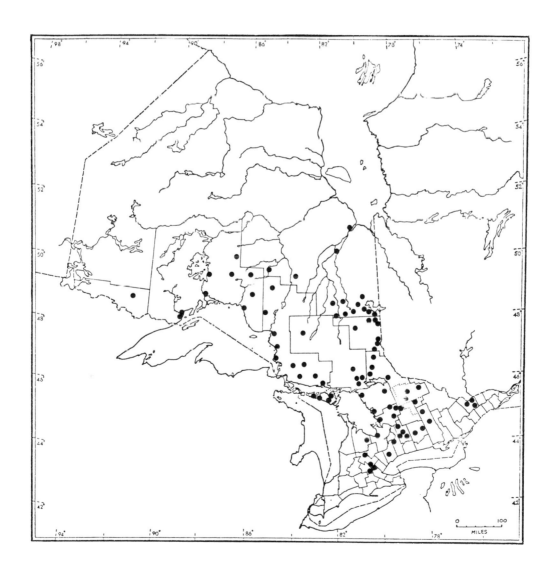

SPECIES: *Colias palaeno* (Linnaeus)

Palaeno Sulphur

TIMETABLE:

Broods   One.

Hibernates   As a half grown larva.

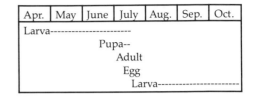

Apr.	May	June	July	Aug.	Sep.	Oct.
Larva----------------------						
		Pupa--				
		Adult				
		Egg				
				Larva----------------------		

OCCURRENCE:

Habitat   Tundra, muskeg and the edges of woods.

Food Plant   Blueberry.

Distribution   Recorded only from the shores of Hudson Bay, James Bay, Lake Attawapiskat and south to Lukinto Lake, just east of Longlac.

Status   S3

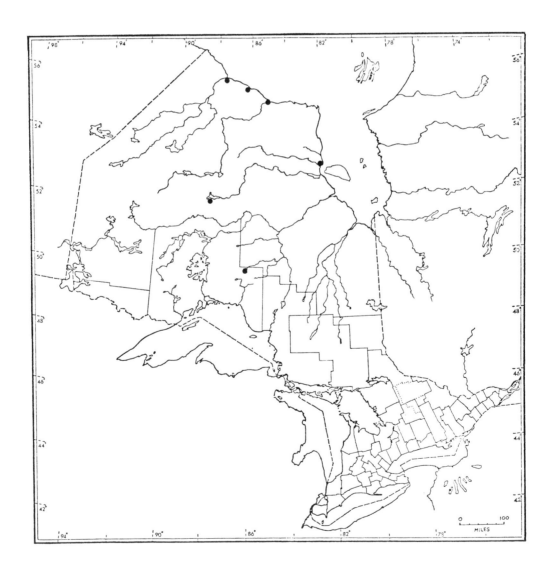

SPECIES: *Eurema lisa* (Boisduval & Leconte)

Little Sulphur

TIMETABLE:

Broods   Two.

Hibernates   Not resident.

OCCURRENCE:

Habitat   Fields, roadsides and open woods, especially where there are flowers.

Food Plant   Partridge pea.

Distribution   An occasional migrant that may be quite widespread in some years, reaching as far north as Algonquin Park and Manitoulin Island, with one record from Westree.

Status   SN

June	July	Aug.	Sep.	Oct.
Immigrant				
Adult-------				
Eggs-----				
Larva---				
Pupa--				
	Adult--------			
	Eggs-------			
	Larva-----			
	Pupa			

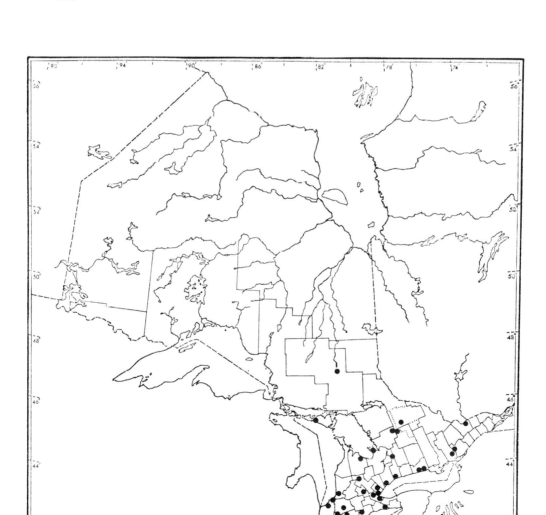

The West Virginia White (*Pieris virginiensis*). Manitoulin Island, May 20, 1975.

A rare stray - The Dainty Sulphur (*Nathalis iole*) at Kettle Point in 1987.

Family: LYCAENIDAE

The Blue, Copper & Hairstreak Butterflies

Life history of the Bog Copper *(Epidemia epixanthe)* from Copetown Bog. Photographed for the first time in 1975 by Walter Plath Jr. Shown are the larva feeding on Cranberry *(Vaccinium macrocarpon)*, the pupa and an adult.

SPECIES: *Feniseca tarquinius* (Fabricius)

The Harvester

TIMETABLE:

Apr.	May	June	July	Aug.	Sep.	Oct.
Pupa------------						
	Adult-------					
		Eggs				
		Larva--				
			Pupa			
			Adult-----			
				Eggs--		
				Larva		
				Pupa----------------		
Some:				Adult-----		
					Eggs	
					Larva	
						Pupa--

Broods   Two, sometimes three in the south.

Hibernates   As a pupa.

OCCURRENCE:

Habitat   Roadsides and edges of damp woods where alders grow.

Food Plant   Larvae are carnivorous, feeding on woolly aphids. These occur primarily on alder, but also on beech, ash, hawthorn, currant and witch hazel.

Distribution Uncommon but widespread over the southerly parts of the province as far north as Matachewan, with several records from around Thunder Bay and Lake of the Woods.

Status   S4

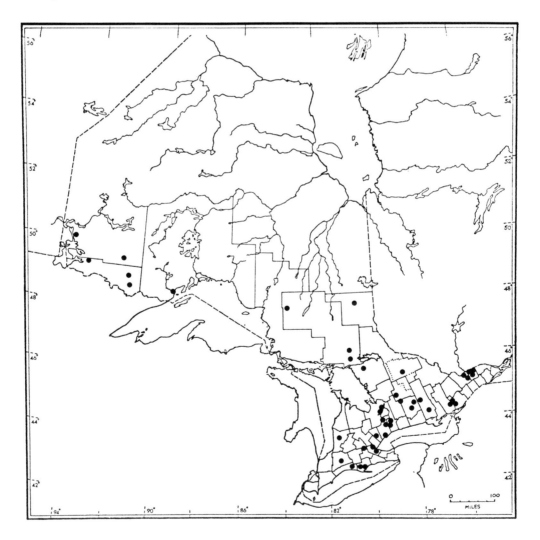

SPECIES: *Lycaena phlaeas* (Linnaeus)

American Copper

TIMETABLE:

	Apr.	May	June	July	Aug.	Sep.	Oct.
Larva-------							
	Pupa-						
		Adult---------					
		Eggs-----					
		Larva-----					
			Pupa				
			Adult---------				
			Eggs----				
				Larva-----------------			
Some:				Pupa-			
				Adult			
				Eggs			
					Larva--		

Broods   Two, and sometimes three in the south.

Hibernates   As a larva.

OCCURRENCE:

Habitat   Fields and open spaces.

Food Plant   Sheep sorrel.

Distribution   Common over the southerly part of the province as far north as the north shore of Lake Huron. A few records further north from Atikokan, Nipigon and Moosonee.

Status   S5

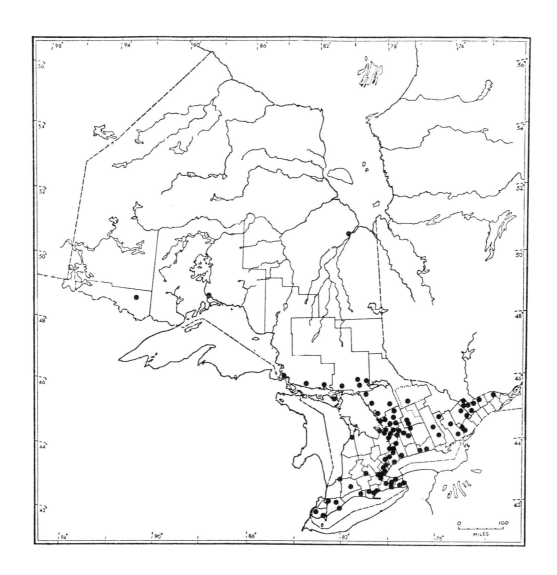

SPECIES: *Hyllolycaena hyllus* (Cramer)   Bronze Copper

TIMETABLE:

Apr.	May	June	July	Aug.	Sep.	Oct.
Eggs---------						
	Larva----					
		Pupa------				
		Adult--------				
			Eggs---			
			Larva---			
			Pupa-----------			
				Adult------		
				Eggs--------------		

Broods   Two.

Hibernates   As an egg.

OCCURRENCE:

Habitat   Fields and open spaces, particularly damp ones.

Food Plant   Water dock, curled dock and smartweed.

Distribution   Widespread and locally common in appropriate habitat over southern parts of the province as far north as Lake Abitibi; also extends west from Nipigon.

Status   S5

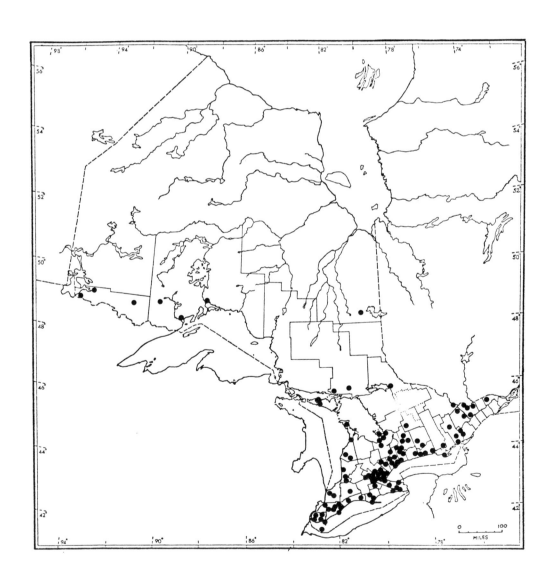

SPECIES: *Epidemia epixanthe* (Boisduval & Leconte)   Bog Copper

TIMETABLE:

Apr.	May	June	July	Aug.	Sep.	Oct.
Eggs---------						
	Larva----					
		Pupa---				
			Adult---------			
				Eggs--------------------------		

Broods   One.

Hibernates   As an egg.

OCCURRENCE:

Habitat   Acid bogs, muskegs and peaty margins of lakes.

Food Plant   Cranberry.

Distribution   Widespread but very local over much of the province south of the Hudson Bay Lowlands.

Status   S5

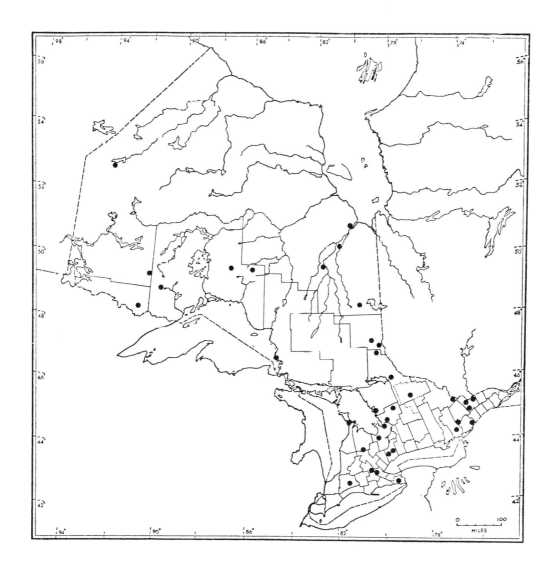

SPECIES: *Epidemia dorcas* (W. Kirby)   Dorcas Copper

TIMETABLE:

Apr.	May	June	July	Aug.	Sep.	Oct.
Eggs-------------						
	Larva----------					
			Pupa			
			Adult---------			
				Eggs--------------------		

Broods   One.

Hibernates   As an egg.

OCCURRENCE:

Habitat   Acid bogs, wetlands and sandy lakeshores where the food plant grows.

Food Plant   Shrubby cinquefoil (*Potentilla*).

Distribution   Widespread but local in the north between the Great Lakes and Hudson Bay. Also frequent along the west side of Bruce County into southwestern Ontario and on Manitoulin and adjacent islands.

Status   S5

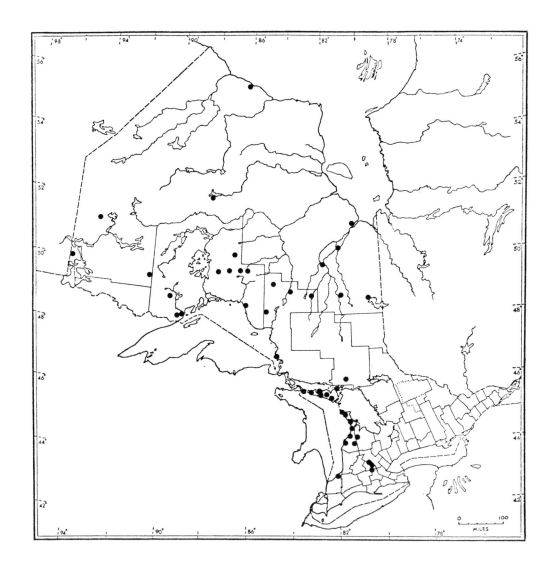

SPECIES: *Epidemia helloides* (Boisduval)   Purplish Copper

TIMETABLE:

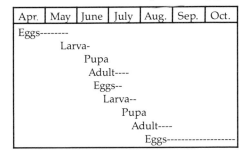

Apr.	May	June	July	Aug.	Sep.	Oct.

Broods   Two.

Hibernates   As an egg.

OCCURRENCE:

Habitat   Dry open areas, especially sandy ones. Also recorded from some acid bogs in the north.

Food Plant   Various docks and knotweeds.

Distribution Recorded from scattered localities in northern Ontario, the north shore of Lake Huron and around the western end of Lake Ontario. One old record from Ottawa. Always local and uncommon, becoming rare and sporadic in the southern part of its range.

Status   S3

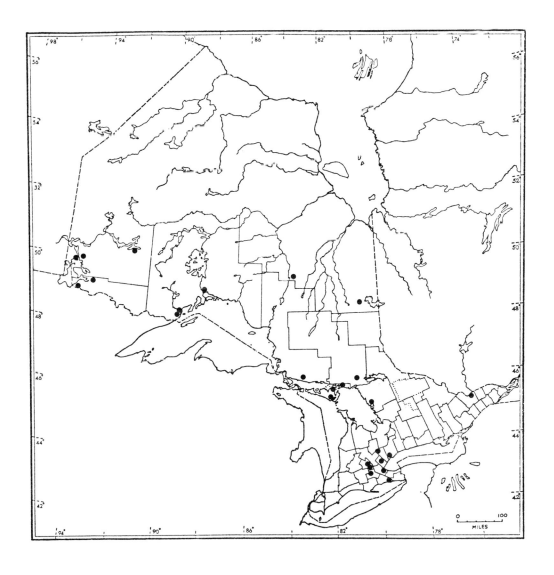

SPECIES: *Harkenclenus titus* (Fabricius) Coral Hairstreak

TIMETABLE:

Apr.	May	June	July	Aug.	Sep.	Oct.
Eggs--------						
	Larva-----					
		Pupa-				
			Adult--			
				Eggs----------------------		

Broods   One.

Hibernates   As an egg.

OCCURRENCE:

Habitat   Fields, roadsides and the edges of woods.

Food Plant   Wild cherries and plum.

Distribution Locally common in the southerly parts of the province as far north as Lake Timiskaming. Also several records from northwestern Ontario.

Status   S5

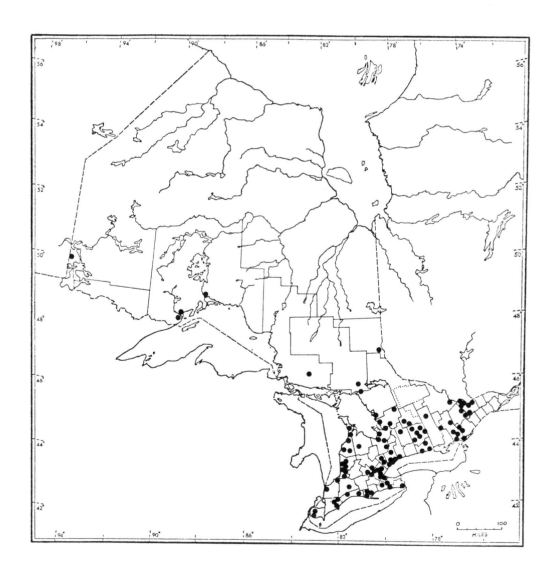

SPECIES: *Satyrium acadicum* (W.H. Edwards)   Acadian Hairstreak

TIMETABLE:

Apr.	May	June	July	Aug.	Sep.	Oct.
Eggs--------						
	Larva------					
		Pupa--				
			Adult			
			Eggs------------------------			

Broods   One.

Hibernates   As an egg.

OCCURRENCE:

Habitat   Fields, roadsides and the edges of woods.

Food Plant   Willows.

Distribution   Common but sometimes sporadic as far north as Sudbury and Lake Timiskaming. Also occurs in the Rainy River District.

Status   S5

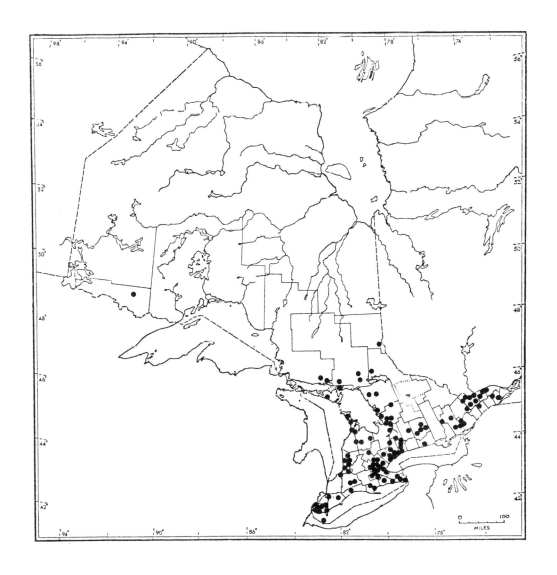

SPECIES: *Satyrium edwardsii* (Grote & Robinson)   Edwards' Hairstreak

TIMETABLE:

Apr.	May	June	July	Aug.	Sep.	Oct.
Eggs--------						
	Larva-----					
		Pupa				
			Adult--			
			Eggs---------------------			

Broods   One.

Hibernates   As an egg.

OCCURRENCE:

Habitat   Roadsides and the edges of woods.

Food Plant   Oaks.

Distribution   Widespread and fairly common in the more southerly parts of the province generally south of the Shield.

Status   S5

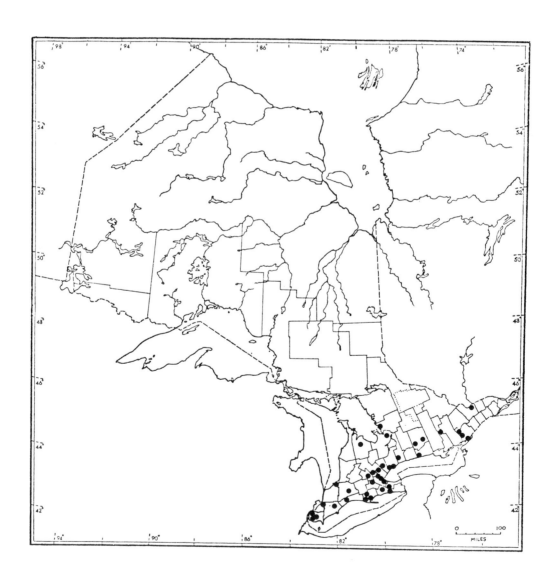

SPECIES: *Satyrium calanus* (Hubner)   Banded Hairstreak

TIMETABLE:

Apr.	May	June	July	Aug.	Sep.	Oct.
Eggs--------						
	Larva------					
		Pupa---				
			Adult----			
				Eggs----------------------		

Broods   One.

Hibernates   As an egg.

OCCURRENCE:

Habitat   Roadsides and the edges of woods, especially where there are flowers.

Food Plant   Oak, walnut and hickory.

Distribution   Widespread and fairly common as far north as Sudbury.

Status   S5

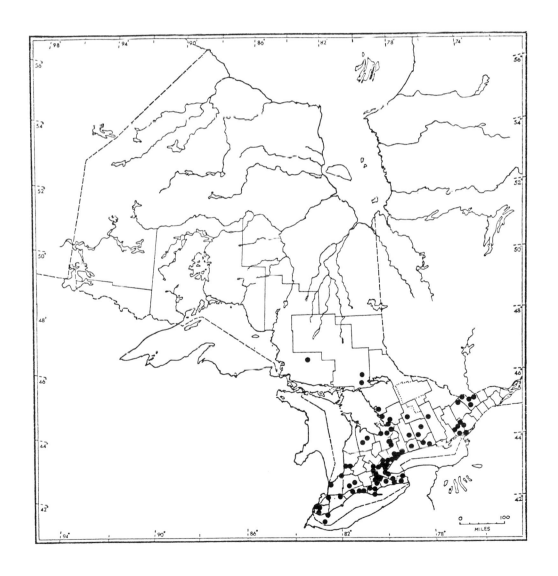

87

SPECIES: *Satyrium caryaevorum* (McDunnough)

Hickory Hairstreak

TIMETABLE:

Apr.	May	June	July	Aug.	Sep.	Oct.
Eggs--------						
	Larva-----					
		Pupa---				
			Adult----			
				Eggs-----------------------		

Broods   One.

Hibernates   As an egg.

OCCURRENCE:

Habitat   Roadsides and the edges of woods.

Food Plant   Hickories.

Distribution Widespread but rather uncommon in the more southerly parts of the province south of the Shield.

Status   S3

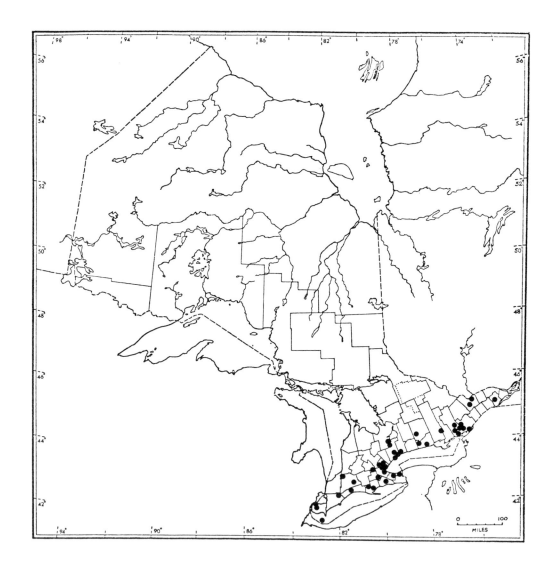

SPECIES: *Satyrium liparops* (Leconte)   Striped Hairstreak

TIMETABLE:

Apr.	May	June	July	Aug.	Sep.	Oct.
Eggs--------						
	Larva------					
		Pupa---				
			Adult---			
				Eggs---------------------		

Broods   One.

Hibernates   As an egg.

OCCURRENCE:

Habitat   Roadsides and the edges of woods especially where there are flowers.

Food Plant   Various members of the heath and rose families.

Distribution   Widespread and sometimes common over the southern and central parts of the
province. In northern Ontario ssp. *liparops* and *fletcheri* have both been recorded into
the Hudson Bay Lowlands.

Status   S5

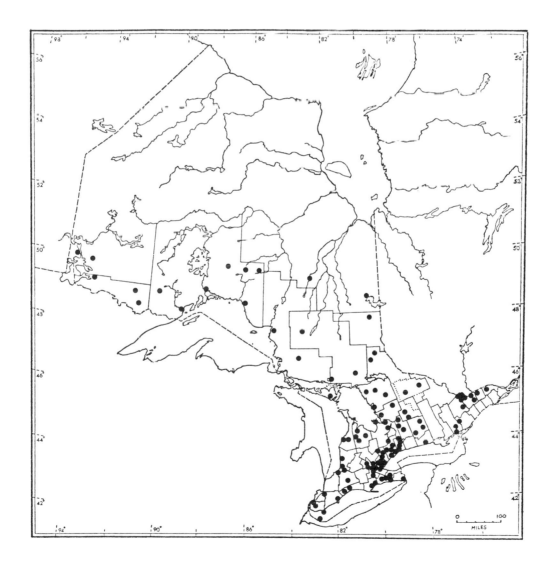

SPECIES: *Mitoura grynea* (Hubner)   Olive Hairstreak

TIMETABLE:

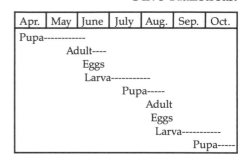

Apr.	May	June	July	Aug.	Sep.	Oct.
Pupa------------						
	Adult----					
		Eggs				
		Larva----------				
			Pupa-----			
				Adult		
				Eggs		
					Larva----------	
						Pupa-----

Broods   Two, but the second may be only partial in some years.

Hibernates   As a pupa.

OCCURRENCE:

Habitat   Open woodlands in the vicinity of its food-plant.

Food Plant   Red cedar.

Distribution   Locally common but apparently confined to Point Pelee and an area towards the eastern end of Lake Ontario.

Status   S3

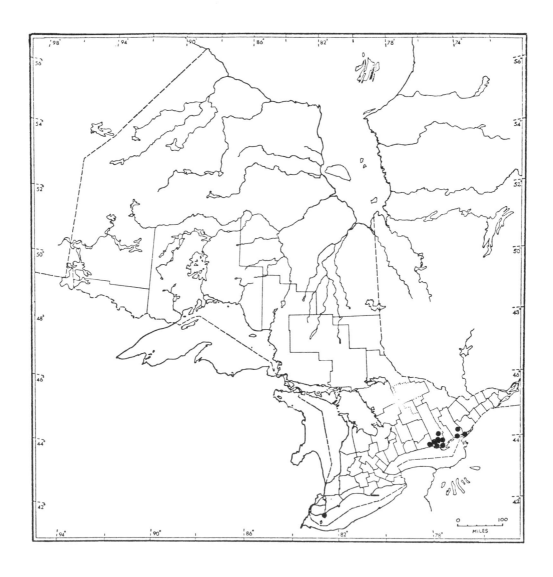

SPECIES: *Incisalia augustinus* Westwood

TIMETABLE:

Broods   One.

Hibernates   As a pupa.

OCCURRENCE:

Habitat   Acid bogs and sandy pine woods in the south, also muskeg and open spaces in the north.

Food Plant   Blueberry, bearberry, Labrador tea.

Distribution   Widely scattered in suitable localities over most of the province.

Status   S5

Brown Elfin

Apr.	May	June	July	Aug.	Sep.	Oct.
Pupa----						
	Adult---					
	Eggs---					
		Larva----------				
				Pupa----------------------		

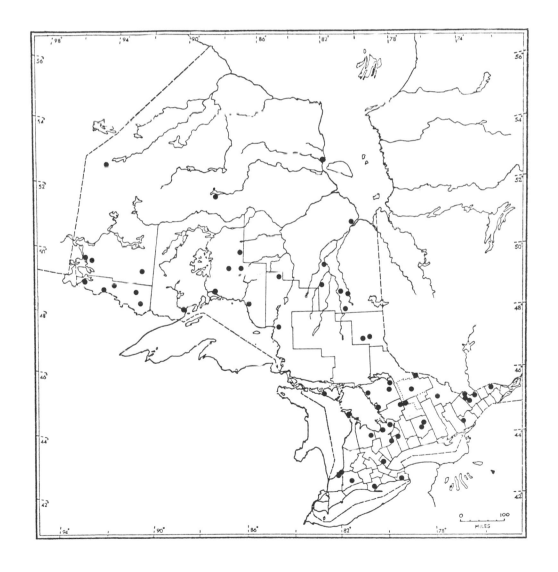

91

SPECIES: *Incisalia polia* Cook & Watson   Hoary Elfin

TIMETABLE:

Apr.	May	June	July	Aug.	Sep.	Oct.
Pupa----						
	Adult---					
	Eggs---					
		Larva-----------				
				Pupa-----------------------		

Broods   One.

Hibernates   As a pupa.

OCCURRENCE:

Habitat   Open spaces with rough scrub and the edges of woods.

Food Plant   Bearberry.

Distribution   Locally common in scattered locations across the province.

Status   S5

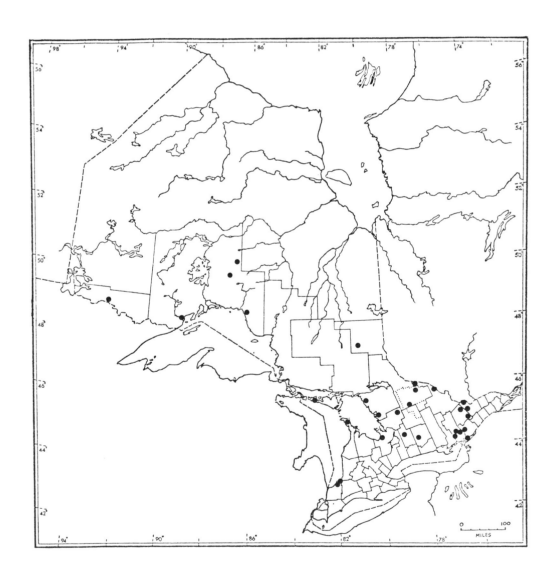

SPECIES: *Incisalia irus* (Godart)　　　　　　　　　　　　　　　　　　　Frosted Elfin

TIMETABLE:

Apr.	May	June	July	Aug.	Sep.	Oct.
Pupa----						
	Adult-					
	Egg--					
		Larva-----------				
				Pupa----------------------		

Broods　　　　One.

Hibernates　　As a pupa.

OCCURRENCE:

Habitat　　　　Woodland trails and open spaces near oak woods with wild lupine.

Food Plant　　Wild lupine and possibly wild indigo.

Distribution　Now very rare and possibly extirpated, it has recently been placed on the Ontario Endangered Species list. Recorded in Pinery Park but not seen there since the 1930's. Recorded uncommonly from a small area in the St. Williams Forest Reserve until the mid 1980's whence its numbers appear to have dwindled to the vanishing point.

Status　　　　S1

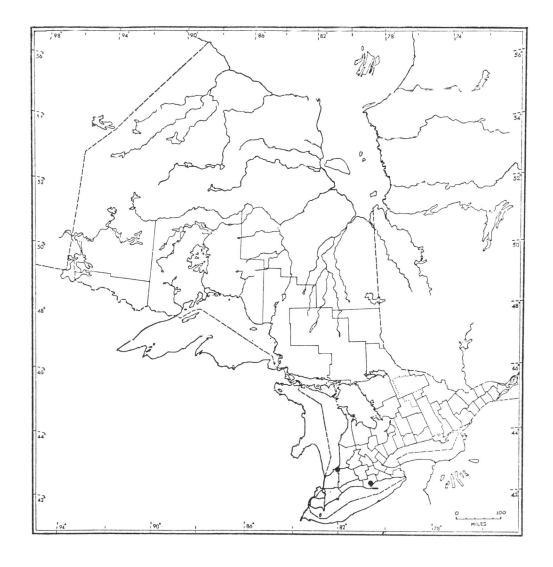

93

SPECIES: *Incisalia henrici* (Grote & Robinson)

Henry's Elfin

TIMETABLE:

Apr.	May	June	July	Aug.	Sep.	Oct.
Pupa---						
	Adult--					
	Eggs--					
		Larva----------				
			Pupa------------------------			

Broods   One.

Hibernates   As a pupa.

OCCURRENCE:

Habitat   Acid bogs, woodland trails and open spaces near woods.

Food Plant   Blueberry.

Distribution Uncommon and very local, recorded mainly from the east of the province and from St. Williams, Muskoka and Manitoulin Island.

Status   S3

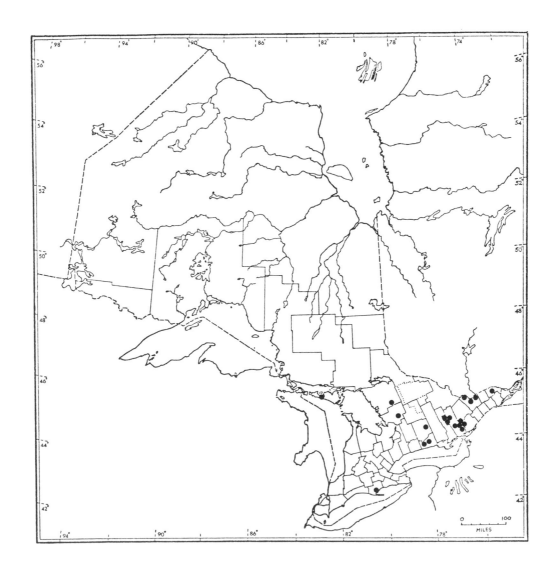

SPECIES: *Incisalia lanoraieensis* Sheppard

Bog Elfin

TIMETABLE:

Apr.	May	June	July	Aug.	Sep.	Oct.
Pupa-------						
	Adult-					
	Eggs--					
		Larva--------				
			Pupa----------------------------			

Broods   One.

Hibernates   As a pupa.

OCCURRENCE:

Habitat   Acid bogs.

Food Plant   Black spruce.

Distribution   Recently discovered in Ontario and known only from the Alfred Bog, east of Ottawa.

Status   Not yet determined.

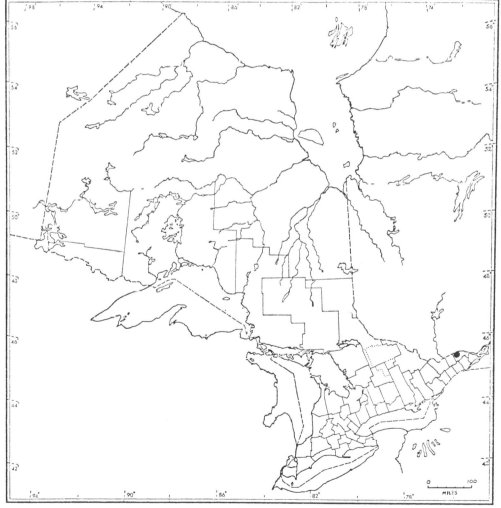

SPECIES: *Incisalia niphon* (Hubner)   Pine Elfin

TIMETABLE:

Apr.	May	June	July	Aug.	Sep.	Oct.
Pupa----						
	Adult----					
	Eggs---					
		Larva-----------			
			Pupa----------------------		

Broods   One.

Hibernates   As a pupa.

OCCURRENCE:

Habitat   Pine woods, woodland trails and open spaces near woods.

Food Plant   White pine and jack pine.

Distribution   Widespread and sometimes common in suitable localities in most parts of the province south of Hudson Bay Lowlands.

Status   S5

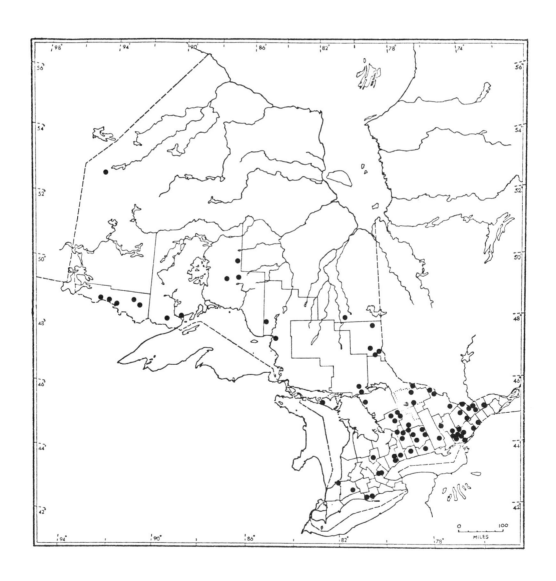

SPECIES: *Incisalia eryphon* (Boisduval)   Western Pine Elfin

TIMETABLE:

Apr.	May	June	July	Aug.	Sep.	Oct.
Pupa----						
	Adult--					
	Eggs-					
		Larva----------				
			Pupa----------------------			

Broods   One.

Hibernates   As a pupa.

OCCURRENCE:

Habitat   Woods, woodland trails and open spaces near woods.

Food Plant   Jack pine.

Distribution   Rare and recorded from only a few scattered localities in the northwestern and central parts of the province.

Status   S4

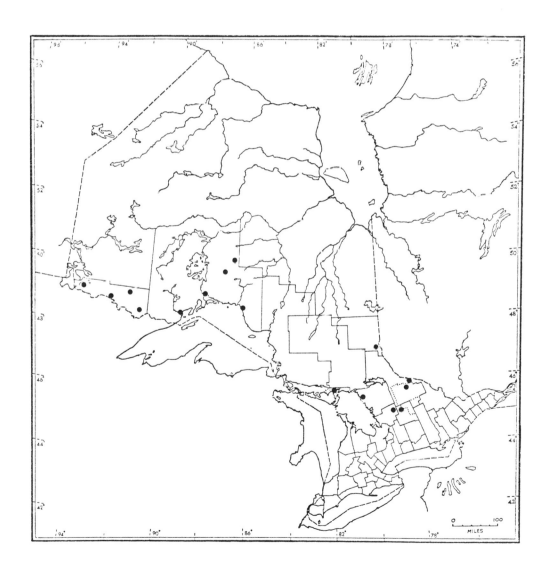

97

SPECIES: *Strymon melinus* Hubner

Gray Hairstreak

TIMETABLE:

Apr.	May	June	July	Aug.	Sep.	Oct.
Pupa-----------------						
	Adult-------------					
		Eggs-----				
		Larva--------------				
			Pupa---------			
			Adult--------------			
				Eggs----		
				Larva---------		
					Pupa--------	

Broods   Two.

Hibernates As a pupa.

OCCURRENCE:

Habitat   Fields and open woodland.

Food Plant   A wide variety of plants but those in the pea and mallow families are perhaps used more frequently.

Distribution Uncommon or rare and scattered over the southern parts of the province as far north as Sudbury and Algonquin Park. Also recently discovered in the Rainy River District.

Status   S3

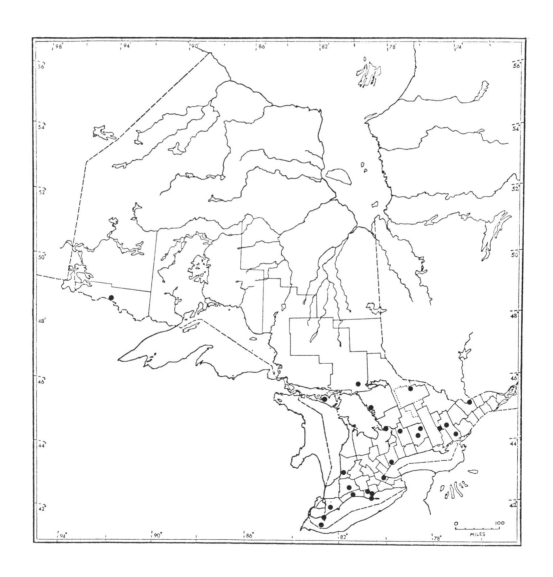

SPECIES: *Erora laeta* (W.H. Edwards)   Early Hairstreak

TIMETABLE:

Apr.	May	June	July	Aug.	Sep.	Oct.
Pupa--------						
	Adult-					
	Eggs					
		Larva------				
			Pupa-----------------------			

Broods   One.

Hibernates   As a pupa.

OCCURRENCE:

Habitat   Woods and woodland trails. It is believed to spend much of its time around the tops of trees.

Food Plant   Beech and beaked hazel.

Distribution   Perhaps very rare and recorded only in a few locations in the southern part of the province.

Status   S3

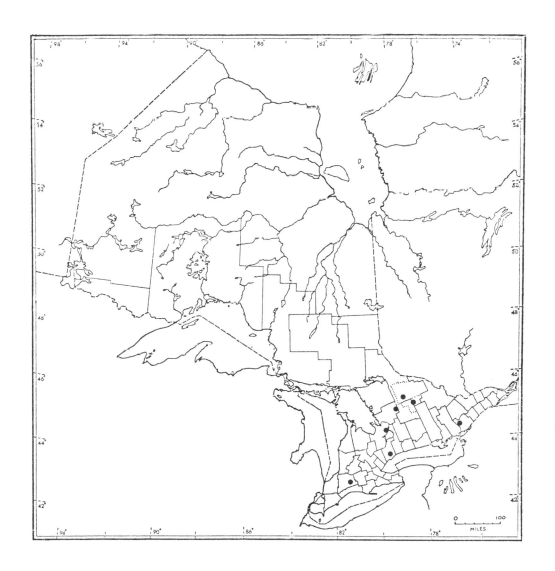

SPECIES: *Everes comyntas* (Godart)   Eastern Tailed Blue

TIMETABLE:

Broods   Two, and sometimes three in the south.

Hibernates   As a larva.

OCCURRENCE:

Habitat   Fields and open spaces.

Food Plant   A wide variety of species in the pea family, particularly vetch and clover.

Distribution Widespread and occasionally common in the southern parts of the province. Scattered records from the north as far as Lakes Nipigon and Abitibi. However, because of the probability of confusion, the northern records may actually be *E. amyntula*. (See under that species).

Status   S5

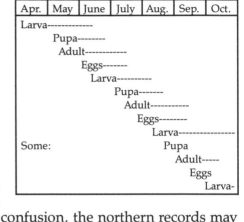

Apr.	May	June	July	Aug.	Sep.	Oct.
Larva------------						
	Pupa--------					
	Adult------------					
		Eggs-------				
		Larva----------				
			Pupa-------			
			Adult-----------			
			Eggs--------			
				Larva----------------		
Some:				Pupa		
				Adult-----		
					Eggs	
					Larva-	

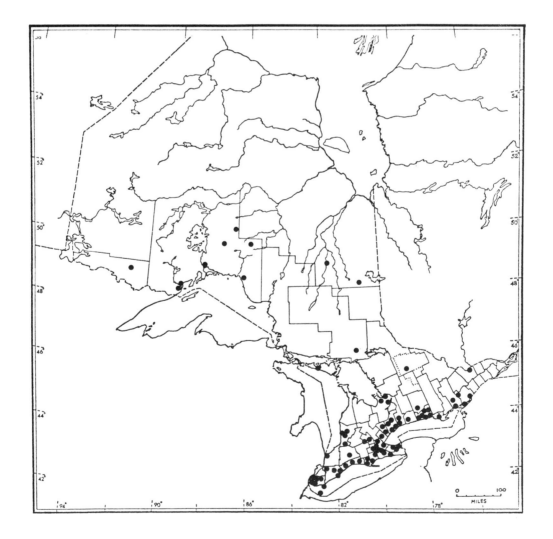

100

SPECIES: *Everes amyntula* (Boisduval)

TIMETABLE:

Broods   One.

Hibernates   As a larva.

OCCURRENCE:

Habitat   Fields and open spaces.

Food Plant   Members of the pea family; wild pea, vetch, locoweed and clover.

Distribution   Widespread and sometimes common north of Lake Superior as far north as Hudson Bay. Isolated records also from the Sudbury-French River area. There may be confusion between *comyntas* and *amyntula*. Geographical separation may be between the western end of L. Superior and L. Timiskaming, with *comyntas* to the south and *amyntula* to the north.

Status   S5

Western Tailed Blue

Apr.	May	June	July	Aug.	Sep.	Oct.
Larva------------						
		Pupa-				
		Adult--				
		Eggs--				
				Larva------------------------		

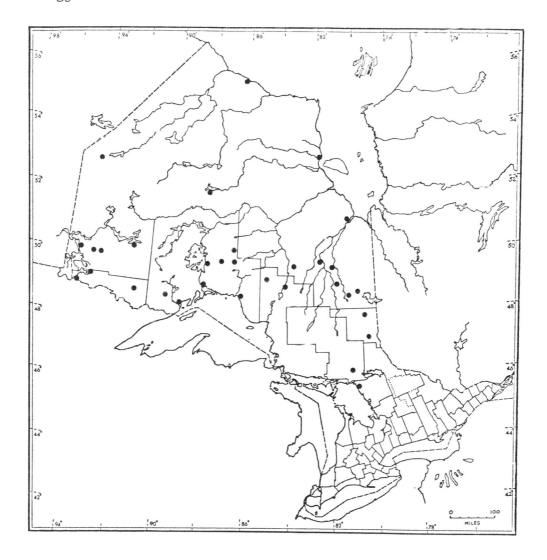

SPECIES: *Celastrina ladon* (Cramer)

Spring Azure

TIMETABLE:

Broods   Two.

Hibernates As a pupa.

OCCURRENCE:

Habitat   Woods, open spaces and fields.

Food Plant A wide variety of plants, including blueberry, meadowsweet, trefoil, sumac, viburnum, wild cherry, oak and dogwood.

Distribution Common almost everywhere south of James Bay. Rarely found however, in built-up areas.

Status   S5

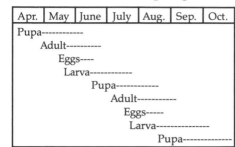

Apr.	May	June	July	Aug.	Sep.	Oct.
Pupa------------						
	Adult----------					
	Eggs----					
	Larva-----------					
		Pupa-------------				
			Adult-----------			
			Eggs-----			
			Larva--------------			
				Pupa-------------		

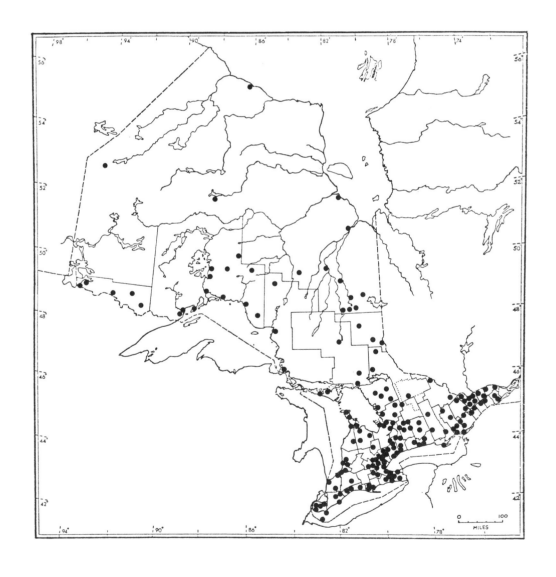

SPECIES: *Glaucopsyche lygdamus* (Doubleday)　　　　　　　　　　　Silvery Blue

TIMETABLE:

Apr.	May	June	July	Aug.	Sep.	Oct.
Pupa--------						
	Adult---------					
		Eggs				
		Larva------------				
					Pupa-----------------	

Broods　　　　One.

Hibernates　　As a pupa.

OCCURRENCE:

Habitat　　　　Woods, woodland trails and nearby open spaces.

Food Plant　　Vetch and white clover.

Distribution　A typically Canadian Zone species occurring mainly on the Shield but ranging as far north as Hudson Bay.

Status　　　　S5

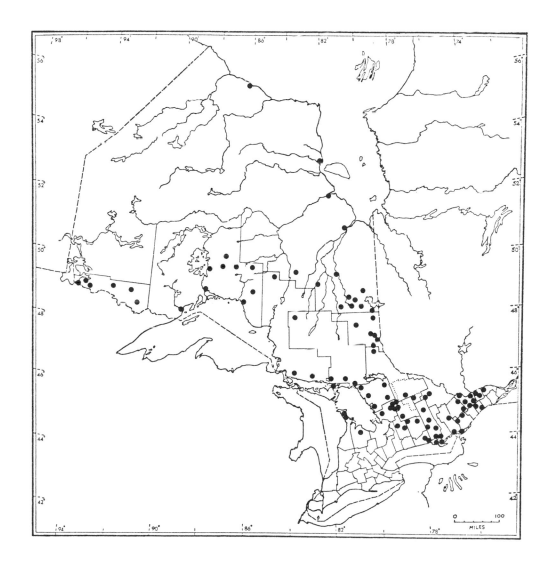

SPECIES: *Lycaeides idas* (Linnaeus)

TIMETABLE:

Broods   One.

Hibernates   As an egg.

Apr.	May	June	July	Aug.	Sep.	Oct.
Eggs---------						
	Larva---------					
		Pupa-----				
		Adult--------				
			Eggs-------------------------			

Northern Blue

OCCURRENCE:

Habitat   Open areas and sandy or rocky woodlands.

Food Plant   Uncertain but probably includes bilberry, black crowberry and Labrador tea.

Distribution Widespread but uncommon in the northern part of the province north of Lake Superior.

Status   S3

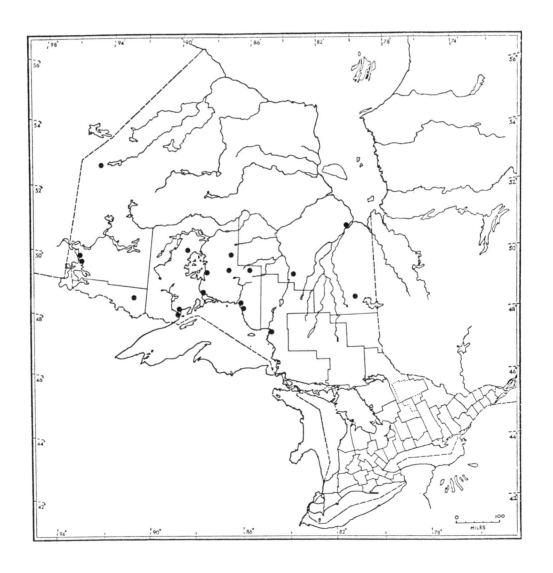

SPECIES: *Lycaeides melissa samuelis* Nabokov

TIMETABLE:

Broods   Two.

Hibernates   As a larva.

OCCURRENCE:

Habitat   Open areas and sandy oak savannah with wild lupine.

Food Plant   Wild lupine.

Distribution   Formerly quite common in three localities in the province - High Park (Toronto), the Pinery south of Grand Bend and the St. Williams Forest. Now very rare and possibly extirpated, it has been recently placed on the Ontario Endangered Species list. It disappeared from High Park about 1926 when weed spraying killed off the wild lupine. It has declined in the other two localities since the mid 1970's, probably through habitat change.

Status   S1

Karner Blue

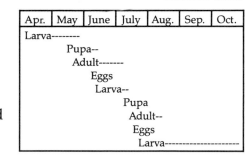

Apr.	May	June	July	Aug.	Sep.	Oct.
Larva--------						
	Pupa--					
	Adult-------					
		Eggs				
		Larva--				
			Pupa			
			Adult--			
			Eggs			
			Larva---------------------			

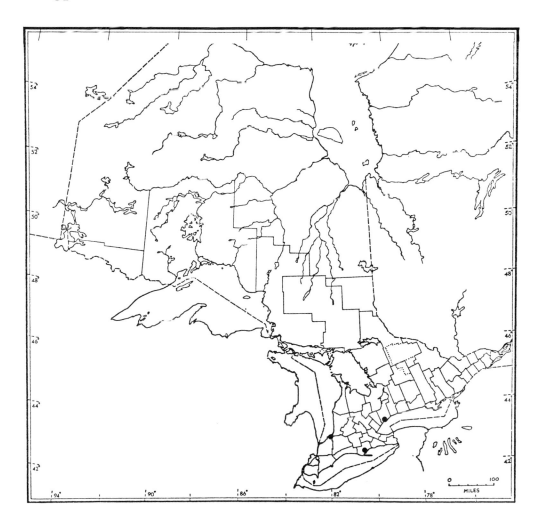

SPECIES: *Plebejus saepiolus* (Boisduval)   Saepiolus Blue

TIMETABLE:

Apr.	May	June	July	Aug.	Sep.	Oct.
Larva-------------						
		Pupa				
		Adult------				
		Eggs--				
			Larva------------------------			

Broods   One.

Hibernates   As a larva.

OCCURRENCE:

Habitat   Roadsides and the edges of woods.

Food Plant   Clover, particularly alsike and white clover.

Distribution   Widespread and sometimes common in the north central parts of the province mainly between the Albany and French Rivers. One record from Waterloo County appears to be a stray since this is well beyond its normal range.

Status   S4

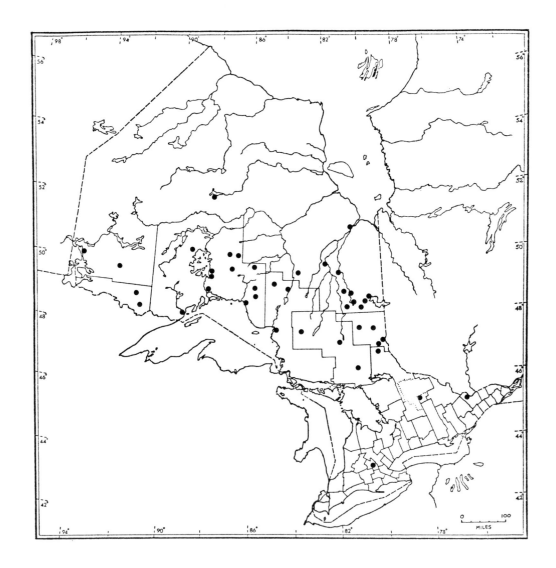

SPECIES: *Agriades rustica* (W.H. Edwards)   Arctic Blue

TIMETABLE:

Apr.	May	June	July	Aug.	Sep.	Oct.
Larva----------------						
		Pupa--				
		Adult				
		Eggs				
				Larva------------------		

Broods   One.

Hibernates   Uncertain but probably as a larva.

OCCURRENCE:

Habitat   Tundra.

Food Plant   Uncertain, probably diapensia, blueberry and saxifrage.

Distribution Only recorded from the edge of Hudson Bay.

Status   S4

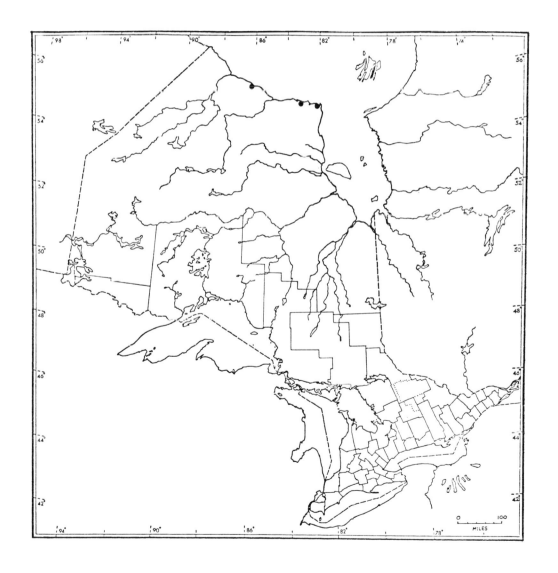

Larvae of The Harvester (*Feniseca tarquinius*) covered by remains of Woolly Aphids near St. Williams (Norfolk Co.) on June 10, 1975.

Ants attending a larva of the Karner Blue (*Lycaeides melissa samuelis*) at the Pinery, July 15, 1984.

Karner Blue adults on Butterfly-weed at the Pinery near Grand Bend, July 25, 1981.

Family: LIBYTHEIDAE

The 'Beak' Butterflies

The Snout Butterfly (*Libytheana bachmanii*) at Point Pelee (Essex County,)
August 11, 1991

SPECIES: *Libytheana bachmanii* (Kirtland)

Snout Butterfly

TIMETABLE:

Broods   Probably two.

Hibernates   Not resident.

OCCURRENCE:

Habitat   Roadsides and the edges of woods, particularly near hackberry trees.

Food Plant   Hackberry.

Distribution   A sporadic but not unusual breeding migrant, mainly in the Carolinian Zone but recorded north to Manitoulin Island.

Status   SN

May	June	July	Aug.	Sep.	Oct.
	Immig.				
	Adult--				
	Eggs				
		Larva-----			
			Pupa		
			Adult		
			Eggs		
				Larva.	

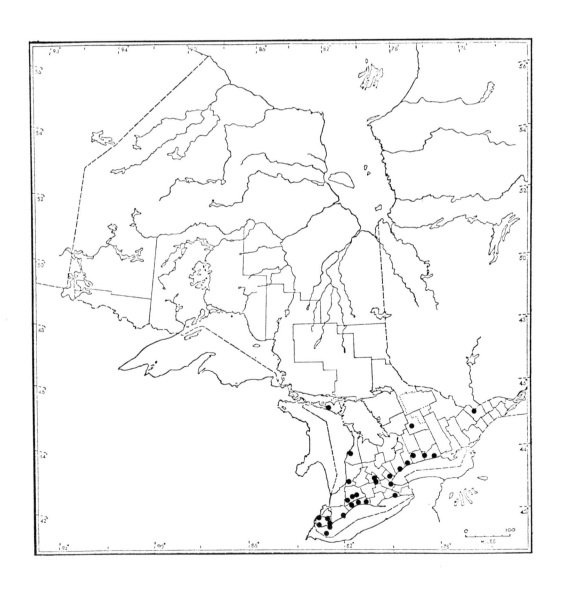

110

Family: NYMPHALIDAE

The Brush-footed Butterflies

The Great Spangled Fritillary (*Speyeria cybele*) at Cambellville (Halton County),
June 7, 1974.

The Hackberry Butterfly (*Asterocampa celtis*) at Point Pelee in 1981.

SPECIES: *Euptoieta claudia* (Cramer)   Variegated Fritillary

TIMETABLE:

	June	July	Aug.	Sep.	Oct.
Immig.					
Adult----					
Eggs--					
Larva---					
Pupa					
Adult					
Some:	Eggs--				
Larva---					
Pupa---					
Adult					

Broods   Two, perhaps a partial third.

Hibernates   Not resident.

OCCURRENCE:

Habitat   Fields, open spaces, roadsides and gardens.

Food Plant   A variety of plants including violets, pansies, flax, may apple, stonecrop and purslane.

Distribution   A sporadic but not unusual breeding migrant which may range occasionally as far north as Lake of the Woods and areas north of Lake Superior.

Status   SN

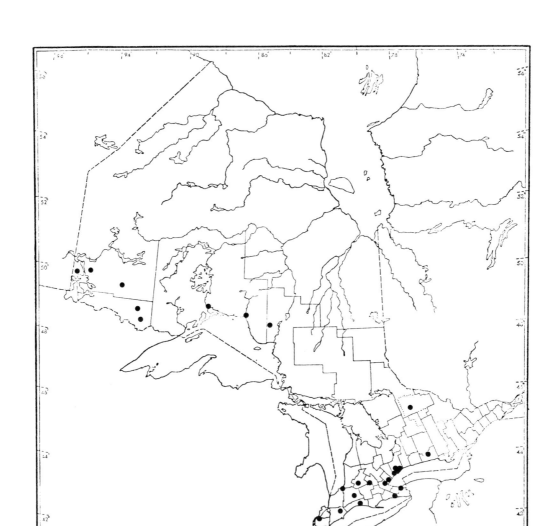

SPECIES: *Speyeria cybele* (Fabricius)

TIMETABLE:

Broods   One.

Hibernates   As a newly hatched larva.

OCCURRENCE:

Habitat   Fields, meadows and around woodlands.

Food Plant   Violets.

Distribution Common in the southern part of the province but sporadic further north. Recorded as far north as Moosonee and the north shore of Lake Superior.

Status   S5

Great Spangled Fritillary

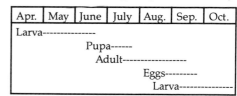

Apr.	May	June	July	Aug.	Sep.	Oct.
Larva---------------						
		Pupa------				
			Adult-----------------			
					Eggs---------	
						Larva--------------

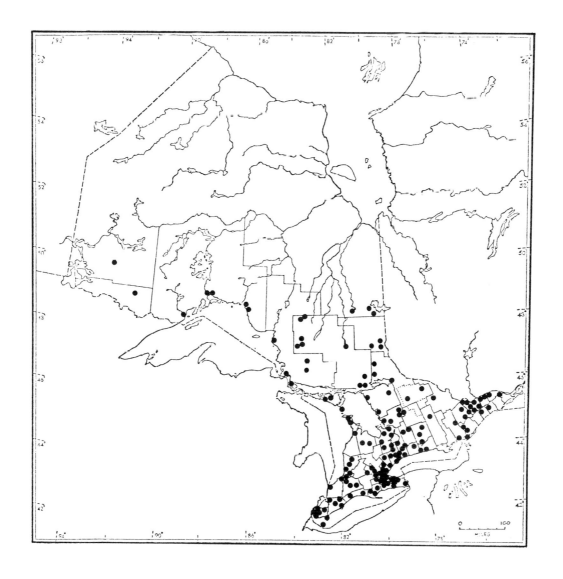

113

SPECIES: *Speyeria aphrodite* (Fabricius)

Aphrodite Fritillary

TIMETABLE:

Apr.	May	June	July	Aug.	Sep.	Oct.
Larva--------------						
		Pupa-------				
		Adult------------				
				Eggs-------		
				Larva--------------		

Broods · · · · · · · One.

Hibernates · · · · As a newly hatched larva.

OCCURRENCE:

Habitat · · · · · · Fields, meadows and around woodlands.

Food Plant · · · · Violets.

Distribution · · · Widespread and recorded as far north as Favourable Lake and James Bay.

Status · · · · · · · S5

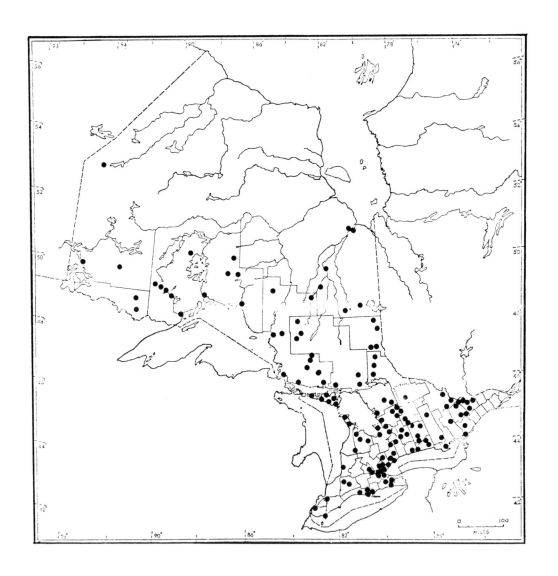

SPECIES: *Speyeria atlantis* (W.H. Edwards) Atlantis Fritillary

TIMETABLE:

Apr.	May	June	July	Aug.	Sep.	Oct.
Larva----------------						
		Pupa------				
			Adult---------------			
				Eggs----		
					Larva------------	

Broods   One.

Hibernates   As a newly hatched larva.

OCCURRENCE:

Habitat   Fields, meadows and around woodlands.

Food Plant   Violets.

Distribution Widespread and recorded as far north as the shore of Hudson Bay.

Status   S5

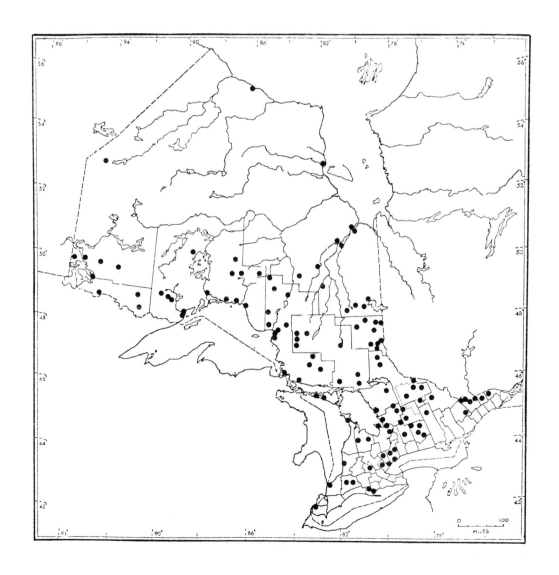

115

SPECIES: *Clossiana eunomia* (Esper)   Bog Fritillary

TIMETABLE:

Apr.	May	June	July	Aug.	Sep.	Oct.
Larva-------------						
		Pupa				
		Adult--				
		Eggs-				
				Larva----------------------		

Broods   One.

Hibernates   As a half grown larva.

OCCURRENCE:

Habitat   Acid bogs.

Food Plant   Willows and alpine smartweed.

Distribution   Locally common throughout the northern parts of the province and recorded as far south as the Mer Bleue Bog near Ottawa and the north part of Hastings County.

Status   S5

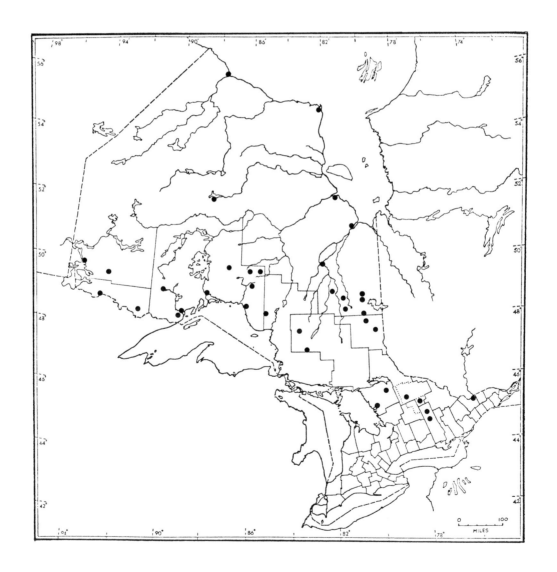

SPECIES: *Clossiana selene* [Den. and Schiff.]

TIMETABLE:

Broods   Two, except in northern parts of the province.

Hibernates As a half grown larva.

OCCURRENCE:

Habitat   Meadows and roadsides, preferring those that are wet and marshy.

Food Plant Violets.

Distribution Widespread and sometimes numerous throughout most of the province.

Status   S5

Silver Bordered Fritillary

Apr.	May	June	July	Aug.	Sep.	Oct.
Larva------------						
	Pupa--					
	Adult-------					
		Larva----------------------------				
Southerly:			Pupa--			
			Adult-------			
			Eggs---			
				Larva------------		

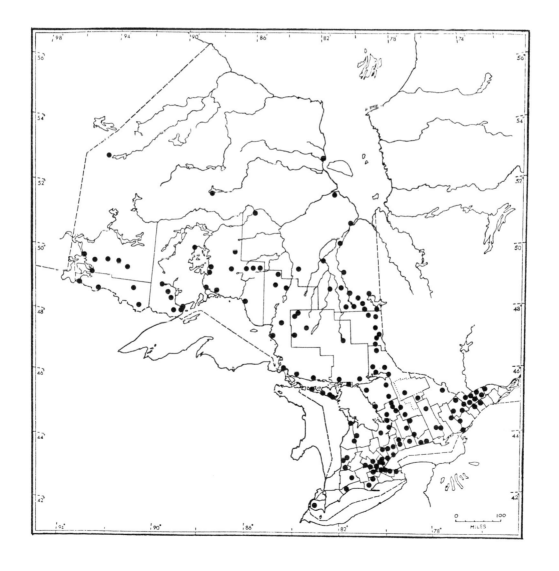

117

SPECIES: *Clossiana bellona* (Fabricius)

Meadow Fritillary

TIMETABLE:

Broods   Two, except in northern parts of the province.

Hibernates   As a half grown larva.

OCCURRENCE:

Habitat   Fields, open spaces and woodland trails.

Food Plant   Violets.

Distribution Widespread and sometimes numerous throughout most of the province south of James Bay.

Status   S5

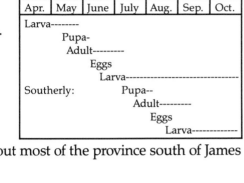

Apr.	May	June	July	Aug.	Sep.	Oct.
Larva--------						
	Pupa-					
	Adult---------					
		Eggs				
		Larva-----------------------------				
Southerly:			Pupa--			
			Adult---------			
				Eggs		
				Larva------------		

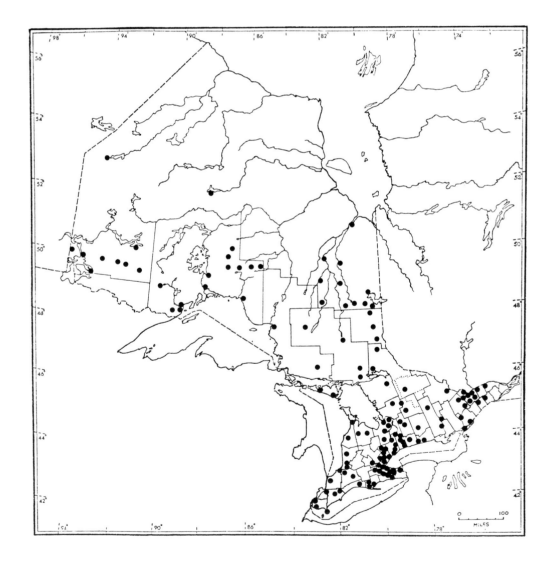

118

SPECIES: *Clossiana frigga* (Thunberg)   Saga Fritillary

TIMETABLE:

Apr.	May	June	July	Aug.	Sep.	Oct.
Larva-------						
		Pupa-				
			Adult			
			Eggs-			
				Larva----------------------------		

Broods   One.

Hibernates   As a larva.

OCCURRENCE:

Habitat   Acid bogs.

Food Plant   Uncertain, probably willows and birches.

Distribution   Primarily a local and somewhat uncommon sub-arctic species recorded as far south as Lake Abitibi and the north shore of Lake Superior.

Status   S4

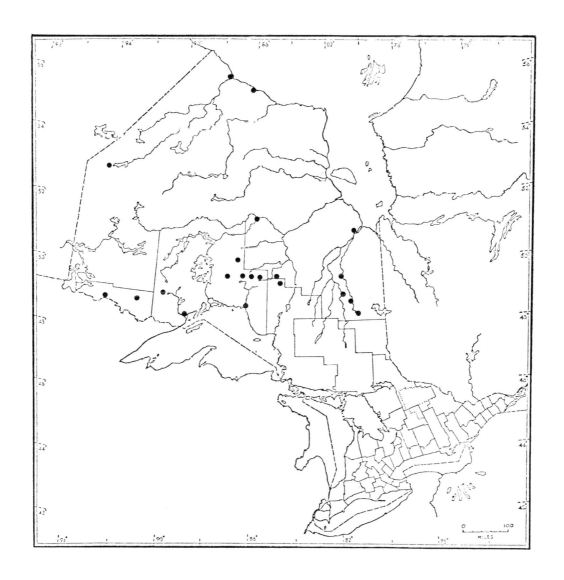

SPECIES: *Clossiana freija* (Thunberg)   Freija Fritillary

TIMETABLE:

Broods   One.

Hibernates   As a larva.

OCCURRENCE:

Habitat   Acid bogs and open pine woodlands.

Food Plant   Uncertain, probably bearberry, billberry and other *Vacciniums*.

Distribution   Local in the northern parts of the province and recorded south to the north shore of Lake Superior and Temagami. One old record from the Mer Bleue Bog near Ottawa.

Status   S4

Apr.	May	June	July	Aug.	Sep.	Oct.
Larva--------						
	Pupa--					
		Adult---				
		Eggs--				
			Larva----------------------------			

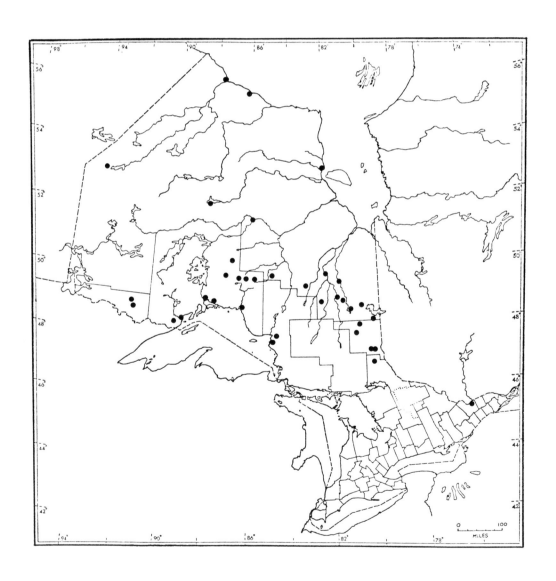

SPECIES: *Clossiana titania* (Esper)   Purple Lesser Fritillary

TIMETABLE:

Apr.	May	June	July	Aug.	Sep.	Oct.
Larva-----------------------						
			Pupa			
			Adult---			
				Eggs--		
					Larva---------------	

Broods   One, but may possibly have a two year life cycle in the far north of the province.

Hibernates   Both times as a larva.

OCCURRENCE:

Habitat   Acid bogs, northern meadows and open pine woodlands.

Food Plant   Dwarf willow and alpine smartweed.

Distribution   Local throughout the northern parts of the province and recorded as far south as the north shore of Lake Huron.

Status   S5

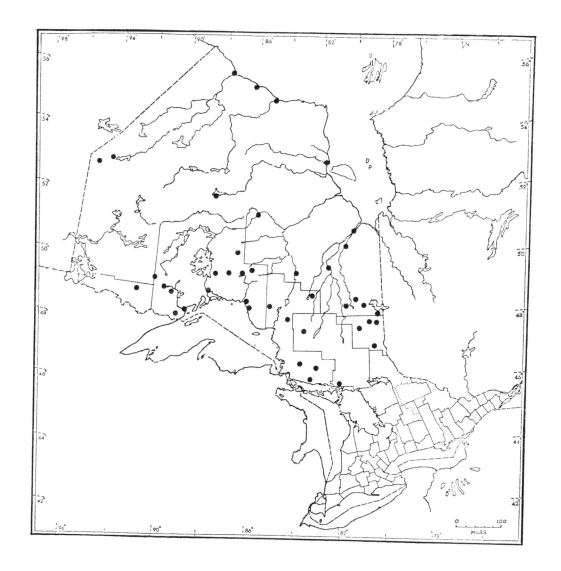

SPECIES: *Charidryas nycteis* (Doubleday & Hewitson)   Silvery Checkerspot

TIMETABLE:

Broods   One.

Hibernates   As a mature larva.

Apr.	May	June	July	Aug.	Sep.	Oct.
Larva--------						
	Pupa-					
		Adult--------				
			Eggs			
			Larva----------------------			

OCCURRENCE:

Habitat   Meadows, grassy areas, and edges of wooded areas.

Food Plant   A variety of composites including sunflowers, asters and coneflower.

Distribution   In local colonies in the south, more widely distributed in the northern parts of the province, as far north as Sioux Lookout and Moosonee.

Status   S4

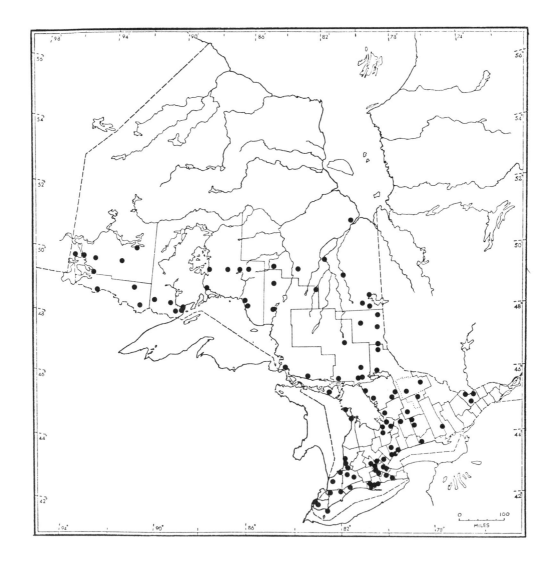

SPECIES: *Charidryas harrisii* (Scudder)   Harris' Checkerspot

TIMETABLE:

Apr.	May	June	July	Aug.	Sep.	Oct.
Larva----------						
	Pupa--					
		Adult----				
		Eggs----				
			Larva-------------------------			

Broods   One.

Hibernates   As a mature larva.

OCCURRENCE:

Habitat   Meadows, particularly those that are wet, and roadsides.

Food Plant   Flat-topped white aster.

Distribution Very local in scattered colonies in the south but more widespread and general further north. Most plentiful in the central parts of the province.

Status   S4

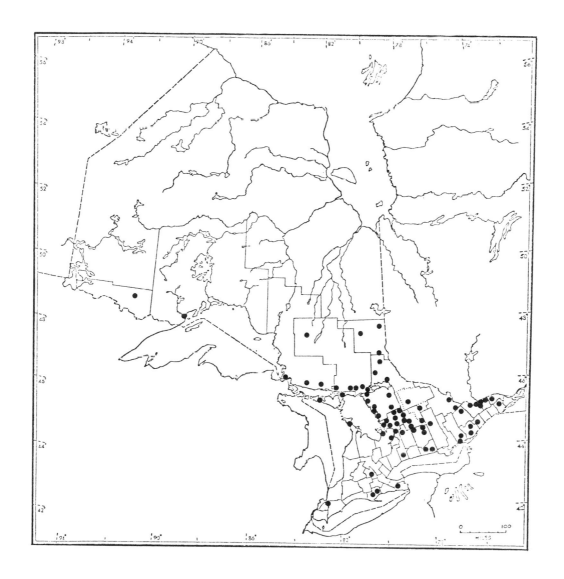

SPECIES: *Phyciodes tharos* (Drury)

Pearl Crescent

TIMETABLE:

Broods   Two, sometimes three in the south. Adults fly continuously from May to October.

Hibernates   As a larva.

OCCURRENCE:

Habitat   Meadows, open spaces, roadsides and the edges of woods.

Food Plant   Smooth-leaved asters.

Distribution Very common and one of the most abundant butterflies, recorded everywhere to the Hudson Bay shore.

Status   S5

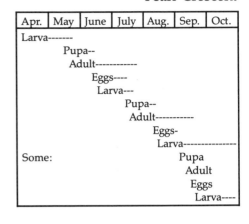

Apr.	May	June	July	Aug.	Sep.	Oct.
Larva-------						
	Pupa--					
	Adult-----------					
		Eggs----				
		Larva---				
			Pupa--			
			Adult-----------			
				Eggs-		
				Larva--------------		
Some:					Pupa	
					Adult	
					Eggs	
					Larva----	

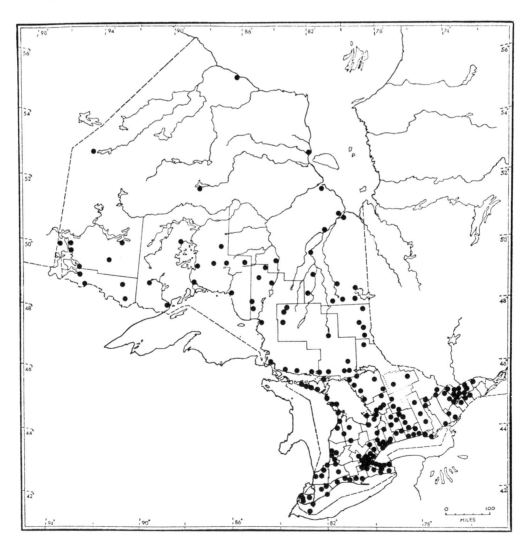

124

SPECIES: *Phyciodes batesii* (Reakirt)   Tawny Crescent

TIMETABLE:

Apr.	May	June	July	Aug.	Sep.	Oct.
Larva-----------						
	Pupa--					
		Adult-----				
		Eggs---				
			Larva-----------------------			

Broods   One.

Hibernates   As a larva.

OCCURRENCE:

Habitat   Open spaces, roadsides and the edges of woods.

Food Plant   Several of the asters, probably prefers the small blue aster.

Distribution   Apparently widespread in local colonies north to the Hudson Bay Lowlands. Although records are not frequent, it may be commoner than it appears since it is probably overlooked or mistaken for *tharos*.

Status   S4

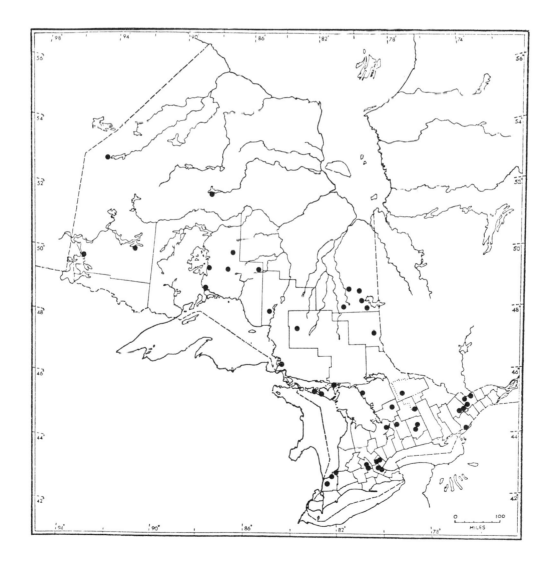

SPECIES: *Euphydryas phaeton* (Drury)

TIMETABLE:

Broods   One.

Hibernates   As a half grown larva.

OCCURRENCE:

Habitat   Stream banks and wet meadows.

Food Plant   Turtlehead. Mature larvae also feed on white ash and common lousewort.

Distribution   In local colonies mainly confined to the south and east of the province. Isolated records also from Sault Ste. Marie and MacDiarmid (Lake Nipigon).

Status   S4

The Baltimore

Apr.	May	June	July	Aug.	Sep.	Oct.
Larva-------------						
		Pupa				
		Adult----------				
			Eggs-----			
			Larva-----------------------			

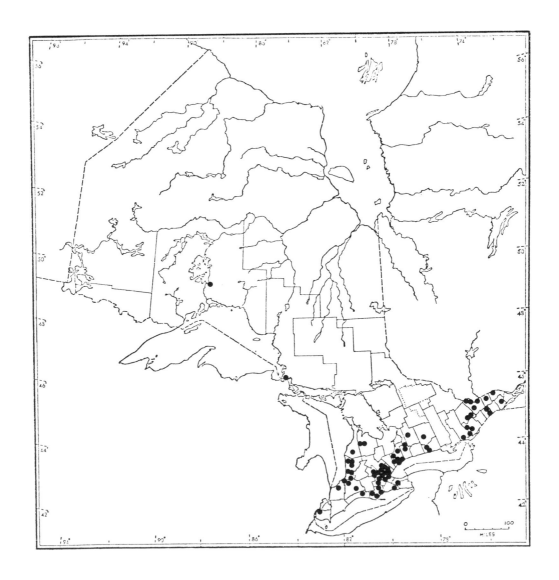

SPECIES: *Polygonia interrogationis* (Fabr.)

Question mark

TIMETABLE:

Apr.	May	June	July	Aug.	Sep.	Oct.
Adult----------------						
	Eggs----					
	Larva---					
		Pupa----				
			Adult----------			
			Eggs---			
				Larva		
				Pupa---		
					Adult-------	

Broods   Two.

Hibernates   As an adult.

OCCURRENCE:

Habitat   Gardens, fields and woods.

Food Plant   Nettles, hops, elms and hackberry.

Distribution   Common and widespread throughout the southern parts of the province as far north as Muskoka and Algonquin Park. Isolated records further north to the latitude of Lake Nipigon.

Status   S5

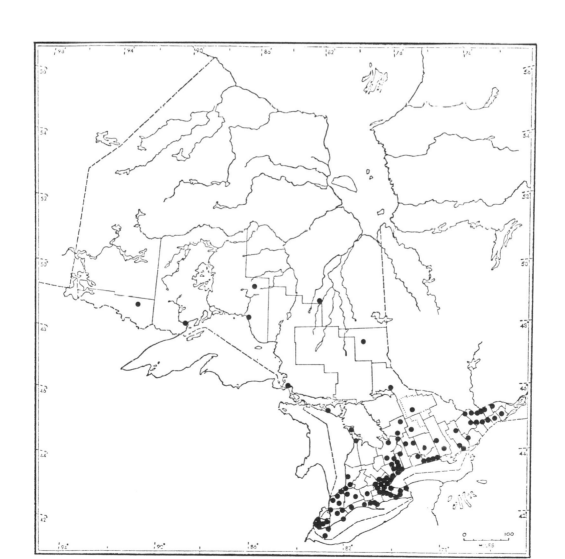

SPECIES: *Polygonia comma* (Harris)

Hop Merchant

TIMETABLE:

Broods   Two.

Hibernates   As an adult.

OCCURRENCE:

Habitat   Woods, woodland trails and adjacent open spaces.

Food Plant   Nettles, hops and elms.

Distribution   Common in the southern parts of the province, rarer northwards but recorded as far north as James Bay and north of Lake Superior.

Status   S5

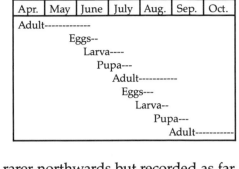

Apr.	May	June	July	Aug.	Sep.	Oct.
Adult-----------						
	Eggs--					
		Larva----				
		Pupa---				
			Adult----------			
			Eggs---			
				Larva--		
				Pupa---		
					Adult----------	

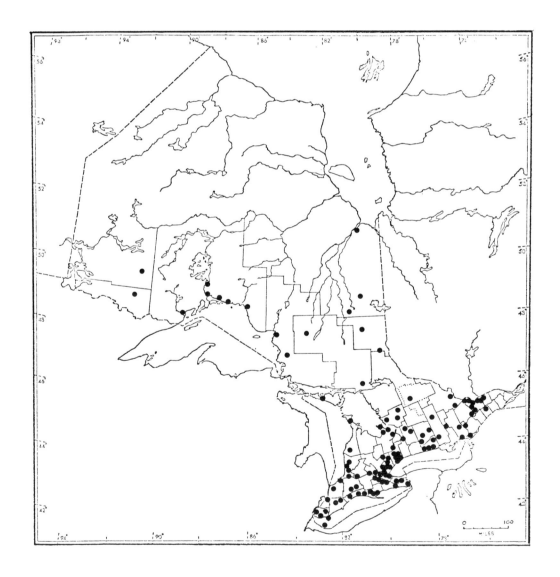

SPECIES: *Polygonia satyrus* (W.H. Edwards)   Satyr Angle Wing

TIMETABLE:

Apr.	May	June	July	Aug.	Sep.	Oct.
Adult----------------						
	Eggs--					
	Larva---					
		Pupa---				
			Adult------------------------			

Broods   Uncertain, but probably one in the east.

Hibernates   As an adult.

OCCURRENCE:

Habitat   Woodland trails and adjacent open spaces.

Food Plant   Nettles.

Distribution   Widespread but rare and only occasionally recorded in the province.

Status   S3

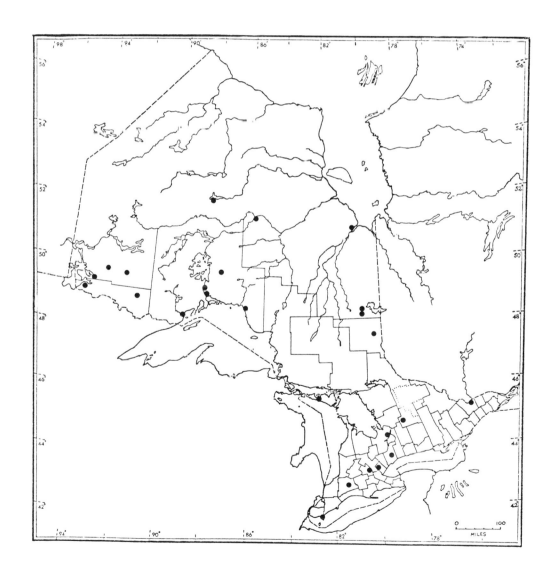

SPECIES: *Polygonia faunus* (W.H. Edwards)   Green Comma

TIMETABLE:

Apr.	May	June	July	Aug.	Sep.	Oct.
Adult--------------						
	Eggs---					
	Larva---					
			Pupa			
				Adult----------------------		

Broods   One.

Hibernates   As an adult.

OCCURRENCE:

Habitat   Woods, woodland trails and adjacent open spaces.

Food Plant   Willows, birches, alders, currants and gooseberry.

Distribution   Widespread over the central parts of the province, more common in the north than in the south, recorded as far north as James Bay.

Status   S4

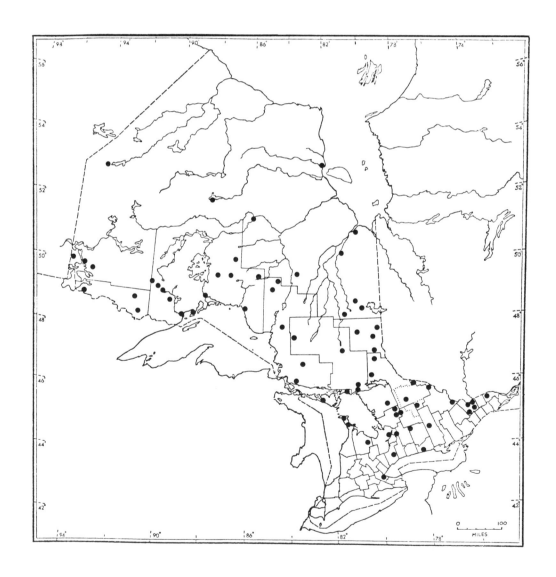

SPECIES: *Polygonia gracilis* Grote & Robinson   Hoary Comma

TIMETABLE:

Apr.	May	June	July	Aug.	Sep.	Oct.
Adult-----------						
		Eggs---				
		Larva--				
		Pupa--				
				Adult------------------------		

Broods   One.

Hibernates   As an adult.

OCCURRENCE:

Habitat   Woods and adjacent open spaces.

Food Plant   Currants.

Distribution   Very rare and only occasionally recorded in the central and northern parts of the
                province.

Status   S3

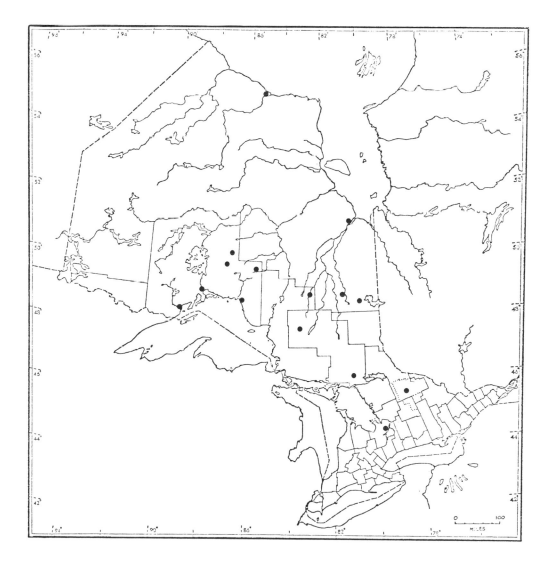

SPECIES: *Polygonia progne* (Cramer)

Gray Comma

TIMETABLE:

Apr.	May	June	July	Aug.	Sep.	Oct.
Adult----------						
	Eggs--					
	Larva---					
		Pupa-				
		Adult-----				
		Eggs----				
		Larva---				
			Pupa			
				Adult-------		

Broods   Two.

Hibernates   As an adult.

OCCURRENCE:

Habitat   Woods, woodland trails and adjacent open spaces.

Food Plant   Currants, birches and elms.

Distribution   Sometimes common and widespread over almost the entire province as far north as James Bay.

Status   S5

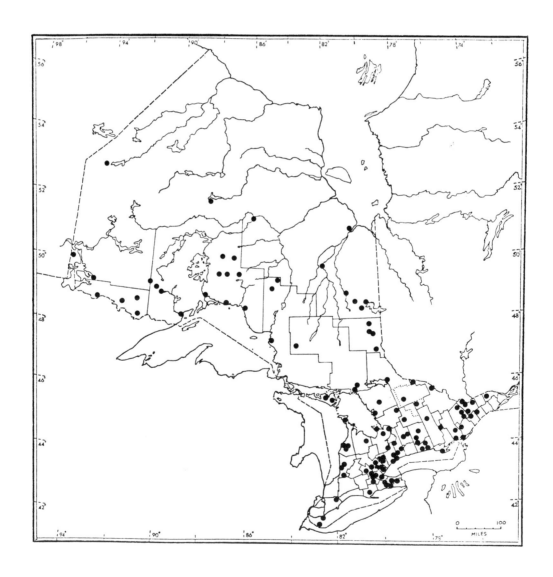

132

SPECIES: *Nymphalis vau-album* ([Den. & Schiff.])

TIMETABLE:

Broods   One.

Hibernates   As an adult.

OCCURRENCE:

Habitat   Mainly woods and woodland trails, but may be found in open spaces and even gardens in the south.

Food Plant   Willows, birches, poplars and alders.

Distribution Widespread throughout the northern, central and southern parts of the province but not recorded from the Hudson Bay Lowlands. Its appearance in southern Ontario is sporadic and it may be absent for several years running.

Status   S5

Compton Tortoiseshell

Apr.	May	June	July	Aug.	Sep.	Oct.
Adult-----------						
	Eggs					
	Larva---					
		Pupa----				
			Adult-------------------------			

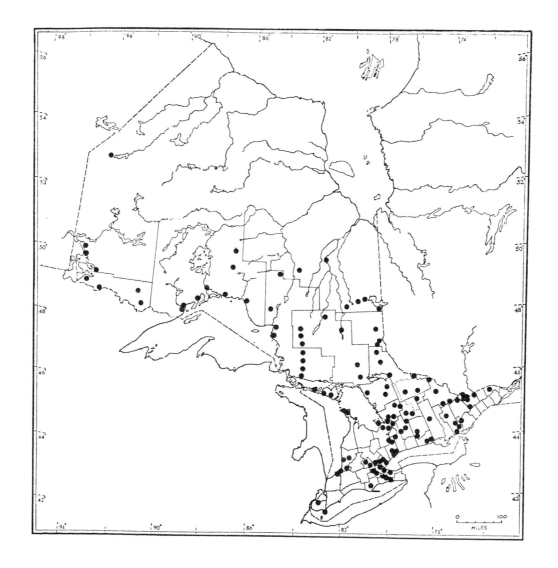

SPECIES: *Nymphalis antiopa* (Linnaeus)

TIMETABLE:

Broods   Two.

Hibernates   As an adult.

OCCURRENCE:

Habitat   Almost everywhere, especially woods, fields and even city gardens.

Food Plant   Willows, poplars, elms and birches.

Distribution   Common throughout most of the province.

Status   S5

Mourning Cloak

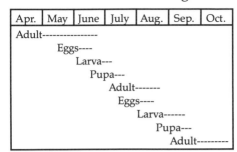

Apr.	May	June	July	Aug.	Sep.	Oct.
Adult---------------						
	Eggs----					
		Larva---				
		Pupa---				
			Adult-------			
			Eggs----			
				Larva------		
				Pupa---		
					Adult--------	

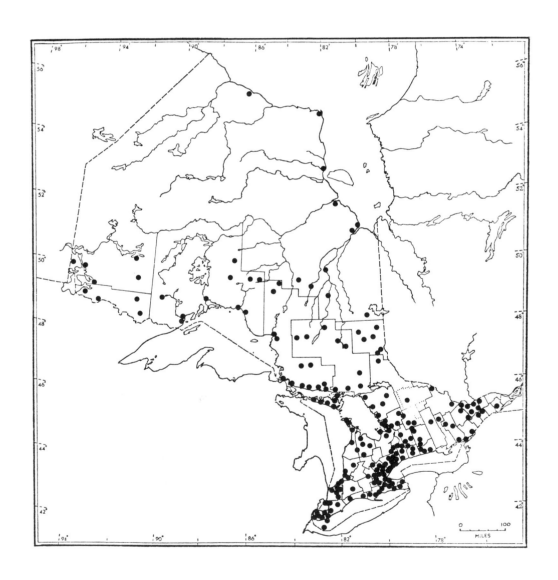

SPECIES: *Aglais milberti* (Godart) Milbert's Tortoiseshell

TIMETABLE:

Broods   Two.

Hibernates   As an adult.

OCCURRENCE:

Habitat   Open spaces and woodland trails.

Food Plant   Nettles.

Distribution   Widespread throughout the entire province.

Status   S4

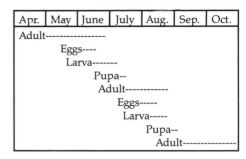

Apr.	May	June	July	Aug.	Sep.	Oct.
Adult-----------------						
	Eggs----					
	Larva-------					
		Pupa--				
		Adult------------				
			Eggs-----			
			Larva-----			
				Pupa--		
				Adult--------------		

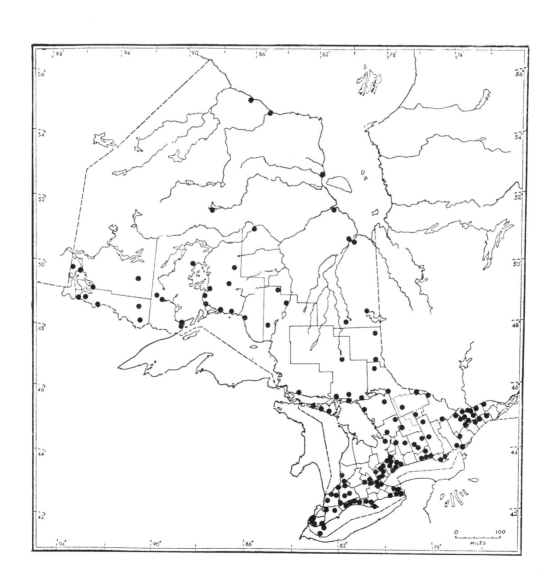

SPECIES: *Vanessa virginiensis* (Drury)

American Painted Lady

TIMETABLE:

Broods   Two.

Hibernates   Probably as an adult. There is uncertainty as to whether it can withstand northern winters or maintains itself by migration.

Apr.	May	June	July	Aug.	Sep.	Oct.
Adult------------						
	Eggs----					
		Larva---				
			Pupa-			
			Adult---------			
				Eggs-----		
				Larva------		
					Pupa------	
						Adult-------

OCCURRENCE:

Habitat   Almost everywhere but especially fields and woods.

Food Plant   Everlastings, wormwoods, burdocks and ironweed.

Distribution   Widespread and common in the south and recorded as far north as Lake of the Woods and to James Bay.

Status   S4

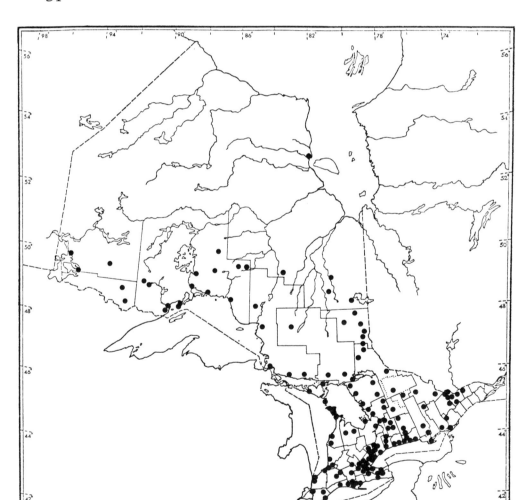

SPECIES: *Vanessa cardui* (Linnaeus)   Painted Lady

TIMETABLE:

Apr.	May	June	July	Aug.	Sep.	Oct.

Broods   Two.

Hibernates   Breeding migrant.

Immigrant
Adult----------
Eggs--
Larva----
Pupa--
Adult----------
Eggs-----
Larva------

OCCURRENCE:

Habitat   Fields, open spaces and roadsides, especially where there are flowers.

Food Plant   Various composites, including thistles, knapweed, burdock, groundsel, sunflower and everlastings.

Distribution A visitor to most parts of the province. Not present every year, in some years only reaching the more southerly parts. Occasionally common and sometimes reaching the Hudson Bay shore.

Status   SN

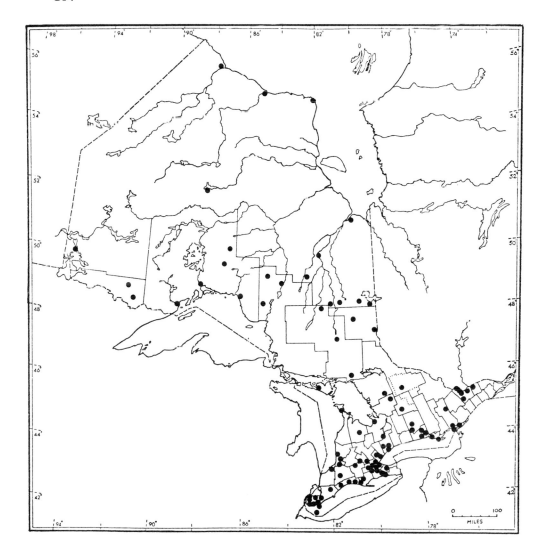

SPECIES: *Vanessa atalanta* (Linnaeus)   Red Admiral

TIMETABLE:

Apr.	May	June	July	Aug.	Sep.	Oct.
Adult-----------------						
	Eggs--					
	Larva-----					
		Pupa-----				
			Adult----------			
			Eggs------			
			Larva----------			
				Pupa------		
					Adult------	

Broods   Two.

Hibernates   As an adult. There is some uncertainty as to
                whether it can withstand northern winters or
                maintains itself by migration.

OCCURRENCE:

Habitat   Almost everywhere, especially woods, fields and
                even city gardens.

Food Plant   Nettles and possibly hops.

Distribution   Common throughout almost all the province. Has noticeable migrations in some areas
                and in some years.

Status   S5

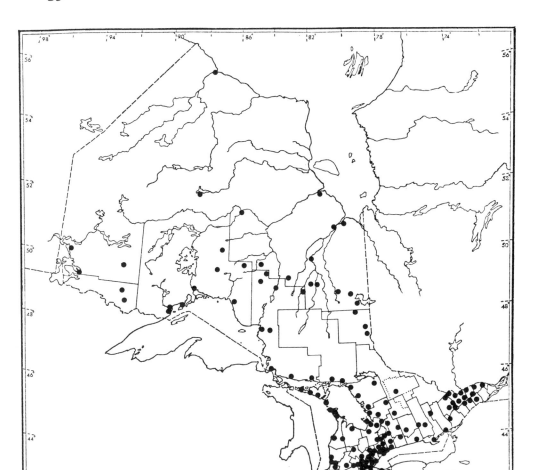

SPECIES: *Junonia coenia* (Hubner)   The Buckeye

TIMETABLE:

Apr.	May	June	July	Aug.	Sep.	Oct.
		Immig.			Immig.	
		Adult			Adult	
		Eggs				
		Larva--				
			Pupa			
				Adult------------		
					Eggs-----	
					Larva	
						Pupa
Possibly:						Adult

Broods   Two and perhaps sometimes three.

Hibernates   Not known to hibernate. However, there is some reported evidence of colonies persisting several years.

OCCURRENCE:

Habitat   Fields, open spaces and roadsides.

Food Plant   Snapdragons, ribgrass, toadflax, plantain and gerardia.

Distribution   A fairly frequent migrant which may range as far north as Algonquin Park and Manitoulin Island. One record from Geraldton, east of Lake Nipigon. It appears mainly in summer though there are a few spring records.

Status   SN

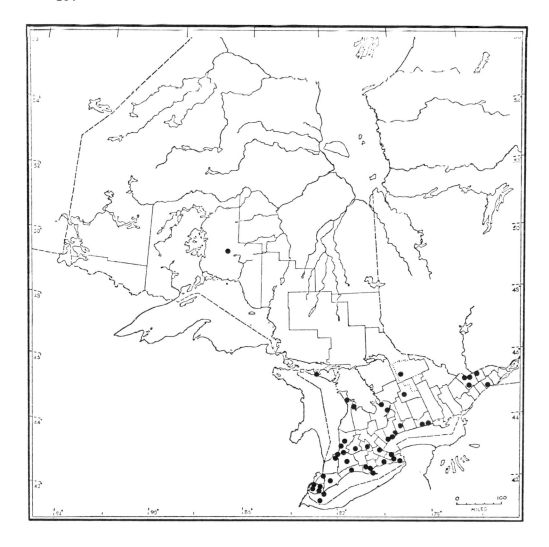

SPECIES: *Basilarchia arthemis arthemis* (Drury)   Banded Purple

TIMETABLE:

Apr.	May	June	July	Aug.	Sep.	Oct.
Larva--------						
	Pupa--					
		Adult----------------				
			Eggs-----			
			Larva----------------------			

Broods   One.

Hibernates   As a half grown larva.

OCCURRENCE:

Habitat   Woods, woodland trails and roadsides.

Food Plant   Poplars and birches.

Distribution Common throughout most of the province except the extreme southwest.

Status   S5

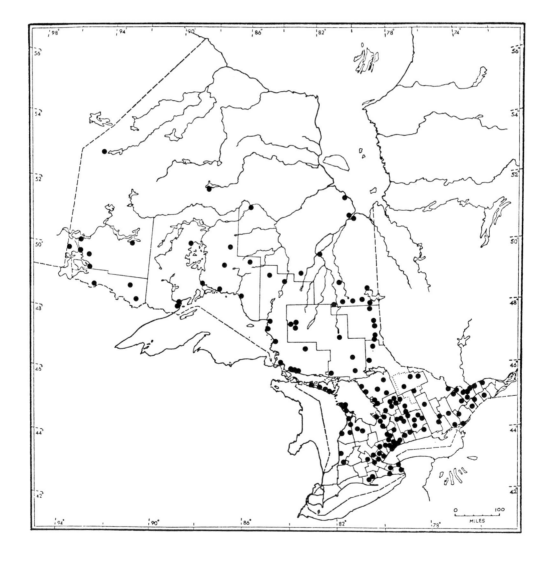

140

SPECIES: *Basilarchia arthemis astyanax* (Fabr.)

Red Spotted Purple

TIMETABLE:

Apr.	May	June	July	Aug.	Sep.	Oct.
Larva---------------						
		Pupa				
		Adult-------------				
			Eggs-------			
			Larva---------------------			

Broods   One.

Hibernates As a half grown larva.

OCCURRENCE:

Habitat   Open spaces and woods.

Food Plant Cherries, poplars and oaks.

Distribution Frequent in the southwestern parts of the province, recorded as far north as Lake Nipissing and east to Northumberland County.

Status   S5

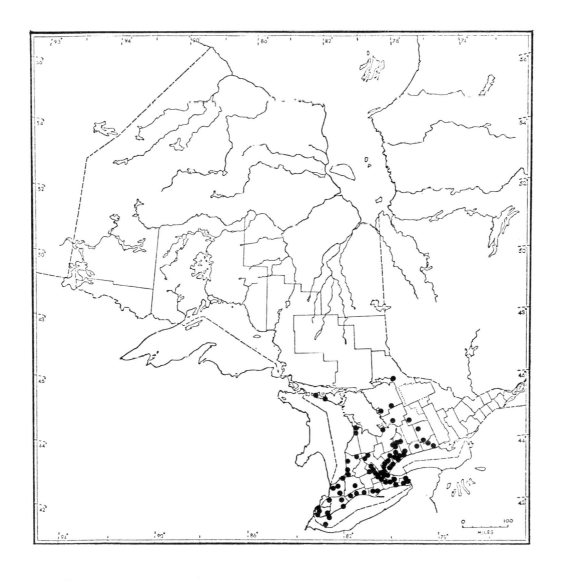

SPECIES: *Basilarchia archippus* (Cramer)   The Viceroy

TIMETABLE:

Broods   Two.

Hibernates   As a half grown larva.

OCCURRENCE:

Habitat   Fields, open spaces and woodland trails.

Food Plant   Willows and poplars.

Distribution   Common in the southern parts of the province. Scattered records from further north
               to Favourable Lake and James Bay.

Status   S5

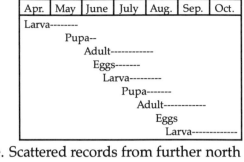

Apr.	May	June	July	Aug.	Sep.	Oct.
Larva--------						
	Pupa--					
	Adult------------					
	Eggs-------					
		Larva---------				
		Pupa-------				
			Adult------------			
			Eggs			
				Larva-------------		

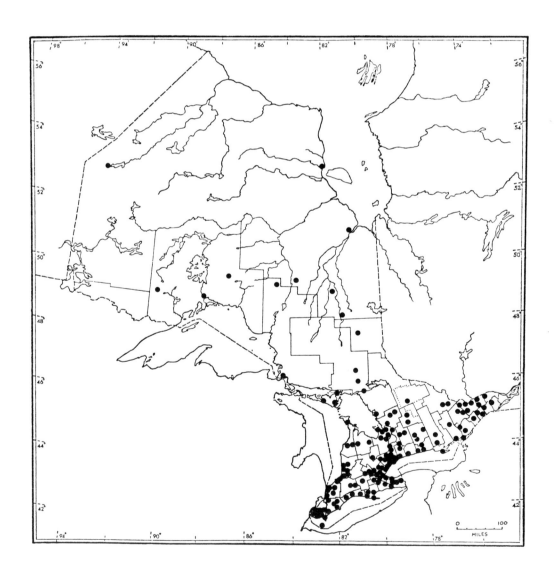

142

SPECIES: *Asterocampa celtis* (Boisduval & Leconte) Hackberry Butterfly

TIMETABLE:

Apr.	May	June	July	Aug.	Sep.	Oct.
Larva------------						
		Pupa				
			Adult---------------			
				Eggs-------		
					Larva---------------------	

Broods   One.

Hibernates As a mature larva.

OCCURRENCE:

Habitat   Open woodland and roadsides where there is hackberry.

Food Plant   Hackberry.

Distribution Fairly common at Point Pelee and Pelee Island, otherwise extremely rare and recorded from few other localities.

Status   S3

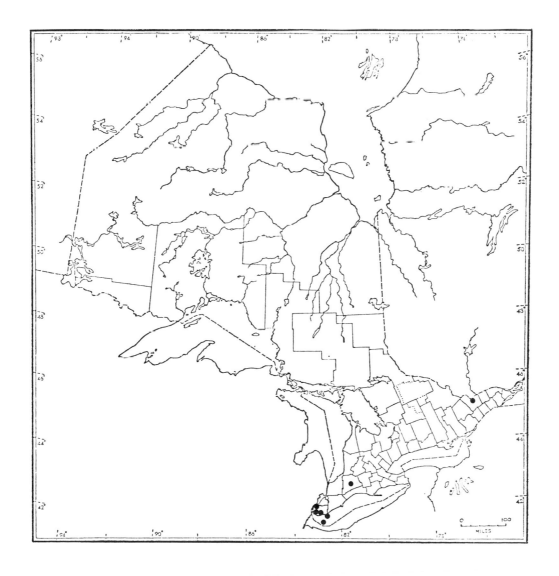

143

SPECIES: *Asterocampa clyton* (Boisduval & Leconte)　　　　　Tawny Emperor

TIMETABLE:

Apr.	May	June	July	Aug.	Sep.	Oct.
Larva-------------						
		Pupa				
		Adult------------------				
				Eggs--------		
					Larva--------------------	

Broods　　　　One

Hibernates　　As a mature larva.

OCCURRENCE:

Habitat　　　　Open woodland and roadsides where there is hackberry.

Food Plant　　Hackberry.

Distribution　Common at Point Pelee. Elsewhere rare and recorded only from scattered localities in southwestern Ontario.

Status　　　　S3

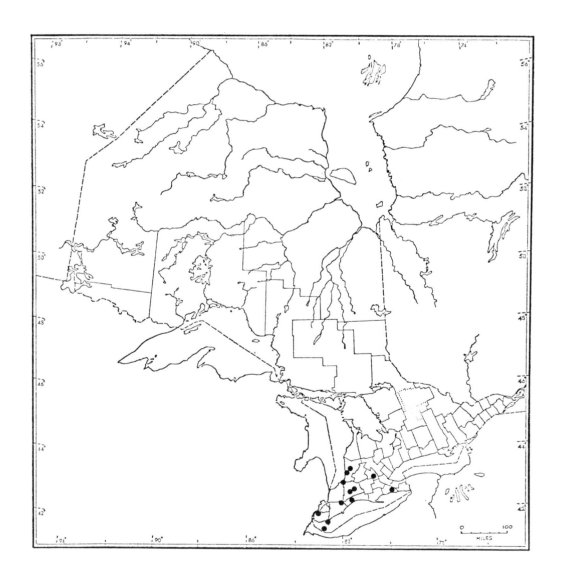

Family: SATYRIDAE

The Brown Butterflies

The Pearly Eye (*Enodia anthedon*) near Campbellville (Halton Co.) in 1974.

The Wood Nymph (*Cercyonis pegala*) near Bobcaygeon (Peterborough Co.) in 1975.

The Jutta Arctic (*Oeneis jutta*) from north of Atikokan (Rainy River Dist.) on June 16, 1972.

SPECIES: *Enodia anthedon* A.H. Clark

Pearly Eye

TIMETABLE:

Apr.	May	June	July	Aug.	Sep.	Oct.
Larva-----------------						
		Pupa				
		Adult-----------				
			Eggs---			
				Larva--------------------		

Broods   One.

Hibernates   As a larva.

OCCURRENCE

Habitat   Edges and interiors of woods.

Food Plant   Grasses, including purple oat and reed canary grass.

Distribution Usually very local in small colonies. Widespread in southern Ontario and recorded from the vicinity of Lake Abitibi westerly to the north of Lake Superior and Lake of the Woods.

Status   S4

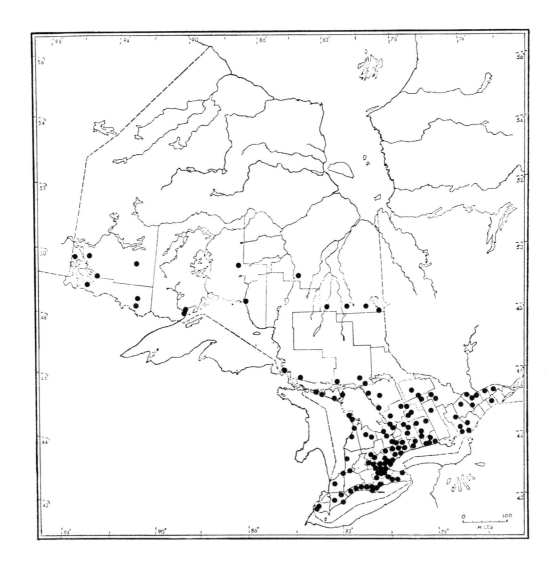

SPECIES: *Satyrodes eurydice* (Johansson)   Eyed Brown

TIMETABLE:

Apr.	May	June	July	Aug.	Sep.	Oct.
Larva----------------						
	Pupa---------					
		Adult---------------				
				Eggs-----		
					Larva----------------------	

Broods   One, with a long flight period of 2-3 months.

Hibernates   As a half grown larva.

OCCURRENCE

Habitat   Grassy areas, particularly in long grass and sedge in open wetlands.

Food Plant   Sedges.

Distribution   Tends to occur in local colonies. Widespread in southern Ontario and recorded generally as far north as Lake of the Woods, Lake Nipigon and Lake Abitibi.

Status   S5

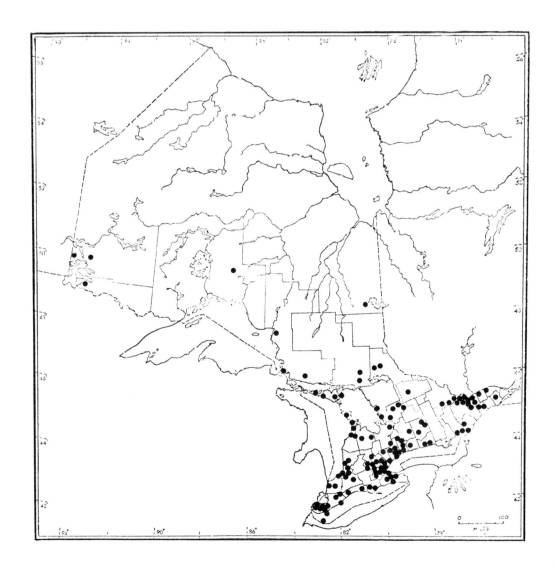

147

SPECIES: *Satyrodes appalachia* (R.L. Chermock)　　　Appalachian Eyed Brown

TIMETABLE:

Apr.	May	June	July	Aug.	Sep.	Oct.
Larva--------------						
		Pupa				
		Adult------------				
			Eggs-----			
			Larva---------------------			

Broods　　　　One.

Hibernates　　As a half grown larva.

OCCURRENCE

Habitat　　　　Grassy areas, particularly within or on the edges of woods near wetland areas.

Food Plant　　Sedges.

Distribution　Southern Ontario, mainly in the Carolinian Zone; also recorded near Lake Simcoe and Ottawa. Since this has been recognized as a separate species only recently, this distribution must be viewed as tentative. The literature states that the distribution is more southerly than that of *S. eurydice* with which it was formerly identified.

Status　　　　S4

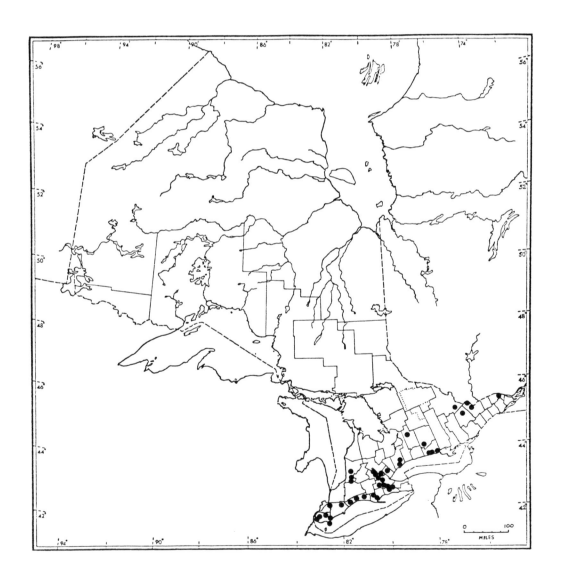

SPECIES: *Megisto cymela* (Cramer)   Little Wood Satyr

TIMETABLE:

Apr.	May	June	July	Aug.	Sep.	Oct.
Larva------------						
	Pupa-----------					
	Adult-----------					
	Eggs------					
		Larva--------------------------				

Broods   One.

Hibernates   As a larva.

OCCURRENCE

Habitat   In or near woodlands and along roadsides, preferring areas with thicker vegetation.

Food Plant   Grasses, including orchard grass and Kentucky blue grass.

Distribution   Widespread and common in the south and recorded north into Timiskaming District and the north shore of Lakes Huron and Superior. Also occurs in Lake of the Woods and Rainy River Districts.

Status   S5

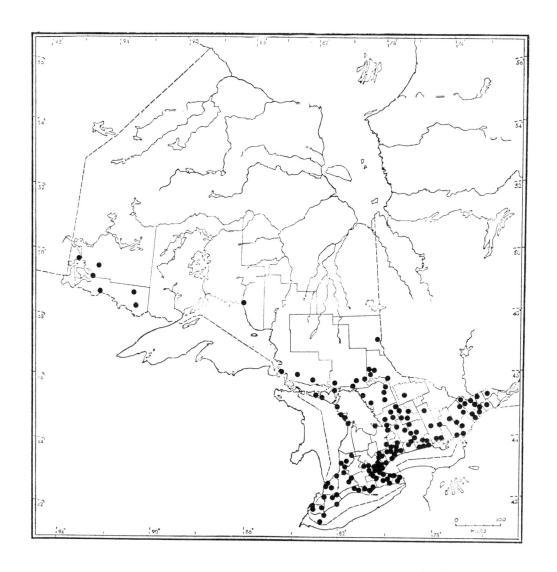

SPECIES: *Coenonympha inornata* W.H. Edwards

Inornate Ringlet

TIMETABLE:

	Apr.	May	June	July	Aug.	Sep.	Oct.
Larva------							
Pupa--							
Adult------							
Eggs							
Northern:			Larva----------------------------				
Elsewhere:			Pupa				
Adult---							
Eggs--							
Larva---------							

Broods — Two, except in northern parts of the province.

Hibernates — As a half grown larva.

OCCURRENCE

Habitat — Open meadows and grassy areas, particularly those that are sandy.

Food Plant — A variety of grasses and sedges.

Distribution — Widespread to the shore of Hudson Bay and often common in the southern parts of Ontario, not recorded from the southwest. It has been expanding its range westerly in southern Ontario in recent years.

Status — S5

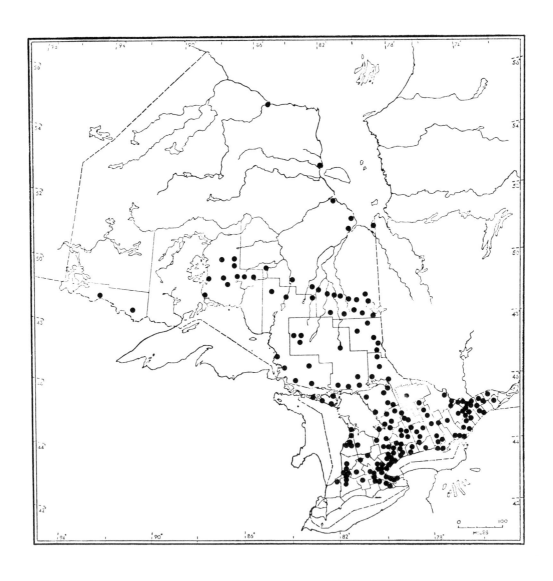

SPECIES: *Cercyonis pegala* (Fabricius)   The Grayling

TIMETABLE:

Apr.	May	June	July	Aug.	Sep.	Oct.
Larva--------------------						
		Pupa-------				
		Adult------------				
			Eggs-----			
				Larva----------------		

Broods   One.

Hibernates   As a newly hatched larva.

OCCURRENCE

Habitat   Fields, open areas and in or near woodlands.

Food Plant   A variety of grasses, including wild oat and purple top.

Distribution   Widespread and common in southern Ontario; recorded north to Lake Abitibi, the
                north shore of Lake Superior and Lake of the Woods area.

Status   S5

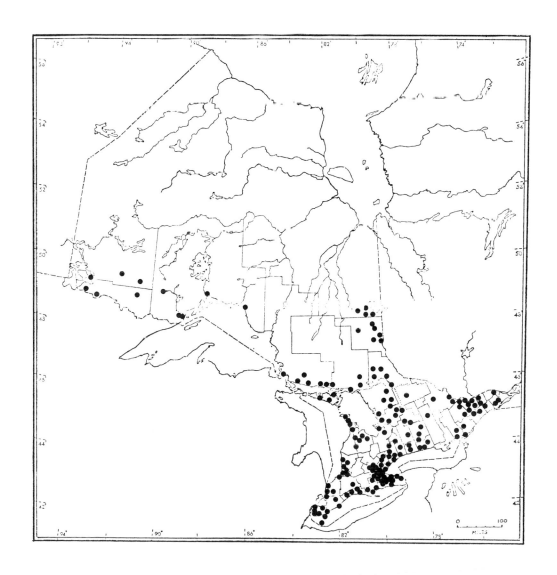

SPECIES: *Erebia disa* (Thunberg) Disa Alpine

TIMETABLE:

Apr.	May	June	July	Aug.	Sep.	Oct.
Larva----------						
	Pupa-					
		Adult---				
		Eggs--				
			Larva------------------------			

Broods   One.

Hibernates   As a larva.

OCCURRENCE

Habitat   Edges of woods and other open spaces in northern forests.

Food Plant   Unknown.

Distribution   Canadian Zone from the north shore of Lake Superior to Favourable Lake, the Albany River and east to Lake Abitibi. Rare and local in northeastern Ontario.

Status   S3

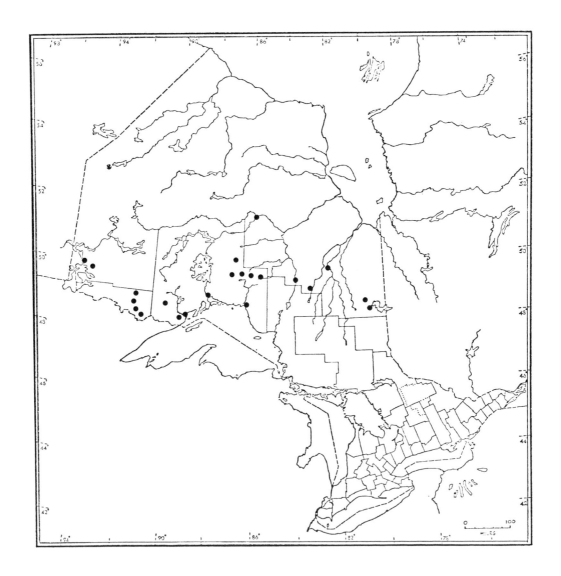

SPECIES: *Erebia discoidalis* (W. Kirby)   Red Disked Alpine

TIMETABLE:

Apr.	May	June	July	Aug.	Sep.	Oct.
Larva----------						
	Pupa--					
	Adult---					
	Eggs					
	Larva-----------------------------					

Broods   One.

Hibernates   As a larva.

OCCURRENCE

Habitat   Edges of woods and other open spaces or wetlands in the northern forests.

Food Plant   Grasses, including Canby's blue grass, alpine blue grass and glaucus spear grass.

Distribution   Canadian Zone, recorded as far south as Sudbury and north to Lake Attawapiskat.

Status   S3

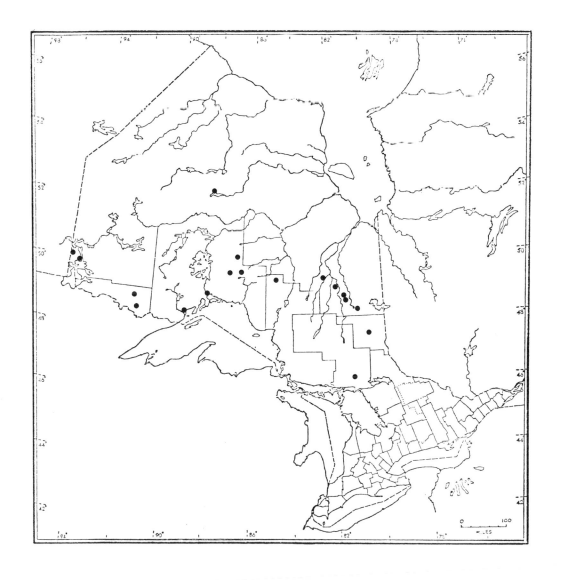

SPECIES: *Oeneis macounii* (W.H. Edwards)

Macoun's Arctic

TIMETABLE:

Apr.	May	June	July	Aug.	Sep.	Oct.
Every second year:						
Larva--------						
		Pupa--				
		Adult---				
		Eggs---				
				Larva-------------------------		

Broods   One, with a two year life cycle. Adults in even numbered years.

Hibernates   As a young larva the first year and a full grown larva the second year.

OCCURRENCE

Habitat   Grassy areas, pine ridges and sometimes acid bogs.

Food Plant   Grasses and sedges.

Distribution   Recorded mainly north and west of Lake Superior and from Algonquin Park.

Status   S3

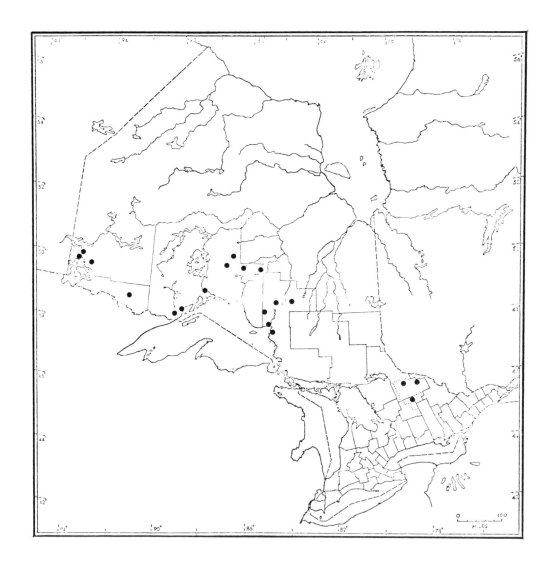

154

SPECIES: *Oeneis chryxus* (Doubleday & Hewitson)   Chryxus Arctic

TIMETABLE:

Apr.	May	June	July	Aug.	Sep.	Oct.
Larva----						
	Pupa					
		Adult---				
		Eggs---				
			Larva---------------------------------			

Broods   One.

Hibernates   As a full grown larva.

OCCURRENCE

Habitat   Open sandy, grassy or rocky areas.

Food Plant   Various grasses, including poverty oat grass, northern rice cut grass and reed canary grass.

Distribution   Appears confined to the Shield and adjacent rocky areas. In these locations it is widespread and sometimes plentiful, becoming rarer and very local northwards. Not recorded west of Lake Superior.

Status   S4

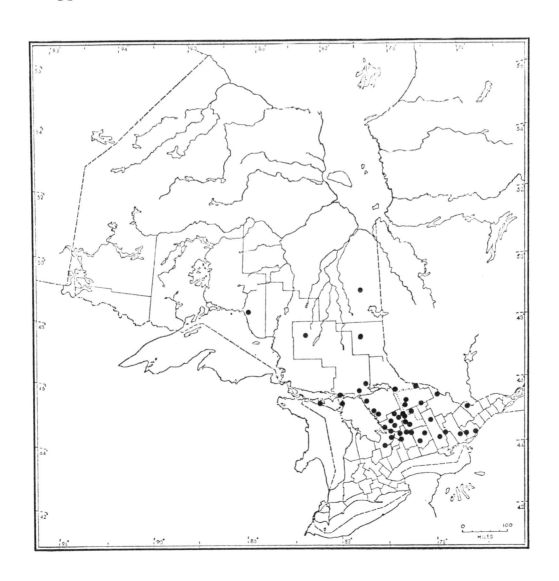

SPECIES: *Oeneis jutta* (Hubner)   Jutta Arctic

TIMETABLE:

Apr.	May	June	July	Aug.	Sep.	Oct.
Larva------						
	Pupa-					
		Adult------				
			Eggs--			
			Larva-------------------------------			

Broods   One.

Hibernates   As a full grown larva.

OCCURRENCE:

Habitat   Acid bogs, muskegs and sometimes drier areas in the Canadian Zone

Food Plant   Cotton grass and rushes.

Distribution   A typically northern and Canadian Zone species recorded from Hudson Bay south
                to Manitoulin Island, Algonquin Park and the Mer Bleue and Alfred Bogs near Ottawa.

Status   S4

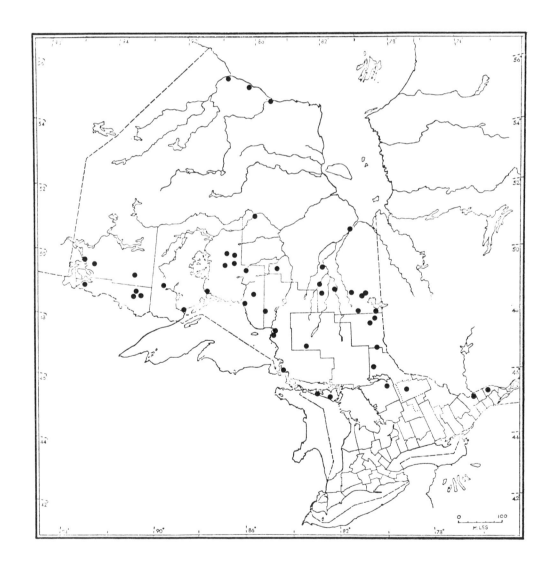

SPECIES: *Oeneis melissa* (Fabricius)　　　　　　　　　　　　Melissa Arctic

TIMETABLE:

Apr.	May	June	July	Aug.	Sep.	Oct.
Every second year:						
Larva----------------						
		Pupa--				
			Adult-----			
			Eggs---			
			Larva------------------			

Broods　　　　　One, with a two year life cycle.

Hibernates　　　Twice, both times as a larva.

OCCURRENCE:

Habitat　　　　　Tundra.

Food Plant　　　Various grasses and sedges.

Distribution　　The shore of Hudson Bay.

Status　　　　　S3

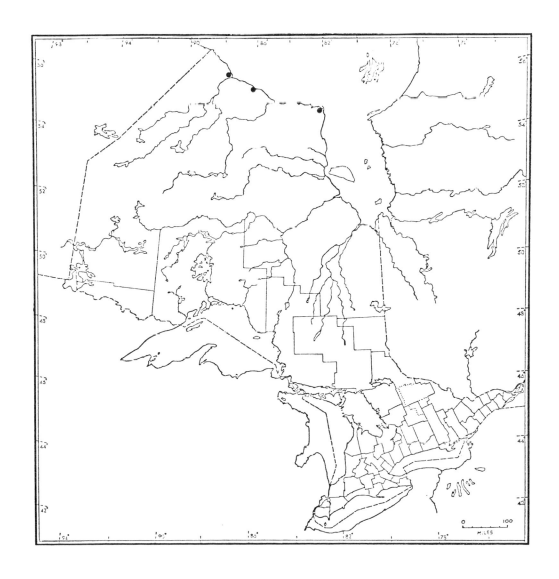

157

The Eyed Brown (*Satyrodes eurydice*) at Campbellville (Halton Co.) in 1975.

Family: DANAIDAE

The Danaid Butterflies

A Monarch larva on Milkweed at North Bay on July 19, 1981.

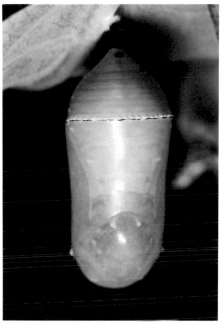

The colourful Monarch pupa on Milkweed.

The Monarch (*Danaus plexippus*) on Butterfly-weed near Grand Bend (Lambton Co.) on July 25, 1971.

SPECIES: *Danaus plexippus* (Linnaeus)

Monarch or Milkweed

TIMETABLE:

Broods   Two and sometimes three in the south.

Hibernates   A breeding migrant. Fall adults migrate southwards.

OCCURRENCE:

Habitat   Any open areas, even in large cities. It may be found almost everywhere except in deep forest.

Food Plant   Various milkweeds, especially common and swamp milkweeds.

Distribution   Arrives almost every spring from the south and spreads northwards. It has been recorded as far north as Lake of the Woods, Lake Nipigon and James Bay. Very common in some years, sparse in others. There is positive evidence for a cycle of abundance peaking about every 11 years.

Status   S4

May	June	July	Aug.	Sep.	Oct.
Immigrant					
Adult----------					
	Eggs				
	Larva----------				
		Pupa------			
		Adult--------------------			
Some:			Eggs-------		
			Larva------		
				Pupa--	
				Adult	

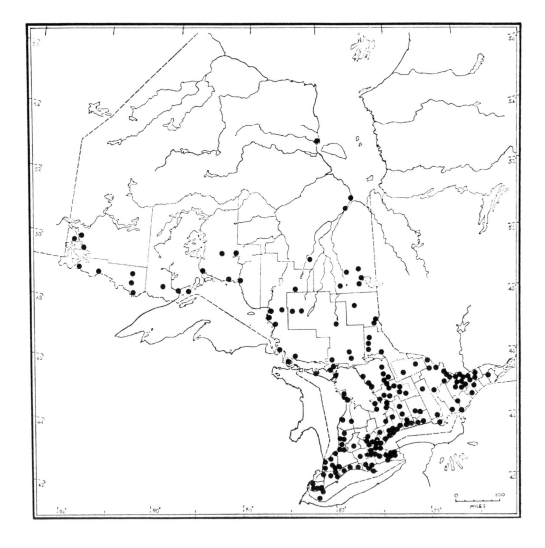

STRAYS

The following species have been recorded in Ontario, mostly substantiated by specimens in the Royal Ontario Museum, the Canadian National Collection or private collections. However, they are of very infrequent occurrence and cannot be considered as either residents or normal migrants.

Achalarus lyciades (Geyer)   Hoary Edge Skipper

Two specimens of this butterfly were taken near Windsor in June and July of 1988. In 1989, a single female was taken at the same location. Not reported in Ontario prior to this and there is insufficient evidence to determine if it is anything other than a stray here. It may be overlooked however, as it is superficially similar to *E. clarus*.

Erynnis zarucco (Lucas)   Zarucco Skipper

A single specimen of this butterfly was taken at Point Pelee on October 6, 1990.

Poanes zabulon (Boisduval)   Zabulon Skipper

Two specimens have been recorded in Ontario. One from Kettle Point (Lambton County) on June 7, 1987 and one at Windsor on June 8, 1990.

Atalopedes campestris (Boisduval)   The Sachem

First taken in London in September 1968. In 1988 there appears to have been a migration into southwestern Ontario with several observed or taken on Pelee Island, Point Pelee and in Windsor. It arrived in June and was observed breeding at Point Pelee with butterflies emerging in August.

Calpodes ethlius (Stoll)   Canna Skipper

A single specimen was recorded at Point Pelee (West Beach) on September 21, 1991.

Panoquina ocola (W.H. Edwards)   Ocola Skipper

A single specimen was recorded in Hamilton (Teaching Gardens) on September 8, 1991 and four specimens at Point Pelee on September 21, 1991.

Eurytides marcellus (Cramer)   Zebra Swallowtail

A rare visitor to the extreme southern parts of the province. All records are from the north shores of Lakes Erie and Ontario west of Port Hope. There is some evidence that it may occasionally breed here for a few years in localities such as Niagara and the extreme southwest where its foodplant, the Pawpaw, is found. The most recent records are of a single specimen taken at Long Point in July, 1974 and two in Essex Co. in 1988, at Point Pelee and Windsor.

Ascia monuste (Linnaeus)   Great Southern White

Recorded as a single stray seen at Point Pelee on June 16, 1981.

Zerene cesonia (Stoll)   Dog Face

A very rare visitor which has been taken as far north as Lake Simcoe. About a dozen occurrences have been recorded and there was a significant migration into the province in 1896. Recent records include Toronto on July 5, 1972 and Windsor on September 17, 1990.

Phoebis sennae (Linnaeus)   Cloudless Sulphur

A rare stray recorded some half dozen times mostly in the extreme southwest of the province. Recent records include Windsor on May 8, 1988 and Toronto on July 25, 1990.

Phoebis philea (Johansson)   Orange Barred Sulphur

A rare stray recorded some half dozen times as far north as Huron County and Toronto. Recent records include Windsor on September 21, 1986 and Toronto on June 15, 1987.

Eurema mexicana (Boisduval)   Mexican Sulphur

A single specimen recorded at Point Pelee on June 28, 1882.

Eurema nicippe (Cramer)   Sleepy Orange

A very rare stray recorded from Point Pelee and Ottawa. It recently occurred in Quetico Provincial Park on June 21, 1978 and at Toronto on May 14, 1990.

Nathalis iole Boisduval   Dainty Sulphur

Two specimens have been recorded in Ontario. One from Bridgenorth near Peterborough in 1947 and one from Kettle Point in 1987.

Gaeides xanthoides (Boisduval)   Great Copper

A single specimen recorded just east of Kenora on July 29, 1979.

Euristrymon ontario (W.H. Edwards)   Northern Hairstreak

This butterfly is a puzzle. The type locality is given as Port Stanley by Klots and as London by Miller & Brown with the holotype as being in the Canadian National collection. Bethune records Port Stanley and a specimen from Grimsby taken in June, 1894. Gibson records two specimens as having been taken at Toronto in 1896. A specimen in the Royal Ontario Museum thought to be *ontario*, labelled as from Toronto but with no data, was found on re-examination, to be *S. calanus*. There is a specimen in the collection of the University of Western Ontario labelled London, Ont., July 1, 1919 (L.E. James). Without further substantiation it cannot be confirmed as a resident.

Parrhasius m-album (Boisd. & Leconte)   White M Hairstreak

Two specimens were recorded from Point Pelee in 1960.

Speyeria idalia (Drury)   Regal Fritillary

A very rare stray in the extreme southwest of the province, recorded on some eight occasions as far north as Toronto. The most recent record was from Langton (Norfolk Co.) in July, 1970.

Charidryas gorgone (Hubner)   Gorgone Checkerspot

Recorded only from London and Toronto in the late 19th century. There are four specimens in the Royal Ontario Museum taken in Scarborough, Toronto on June 6, 1891.

* * * * * * * * * * * * * * * * * * * *

UNCONFIRMED SPECIES

Calephelis muticum McAlpine   Swamp Metalmark

Found in widely distributed localities west of Detroit and Lake St. Clair, this species may occur in southwestern Ontario. It is a distinctive butterfly and should be looked for in wet meadows and swamps where it flies in late July and August.

Clossiana polaris (Boisduval)   Polar Fritillary

Commonly found at Churchill, Manitoba, this subarctic species may range into Ontario along the edge of Hudson Bay.

Neonympha mitchellii French   Mitchell's Satyr

This species is found west of Detroit where it is local in distribution with a short flight season in early July. It occurs in tamarack and poison sumac swamps and could occur in southwestern Ontario.

Oeneis taygete Geyer   White Veined Arctic

Known from the east side of James Bay, P.Q., this subarctic species probably occurs on the Hudson Bay shore in Ontario. It is also found in the Gaspe, P.Q.

Oeneis polixenes (Fabricius)   Polixenes Arctic

Found at Churchill, Manitoba, this subarctic species has been reported from Cape Henrietta Maria but the report requires substantiating. It is quite likely to occur along the Hudson Bay shore.

* * * * * * * * * * * * * * * * * * *

DOUBTFUL SPECIES

A number of species have been recorded from time to time which have normal ranges far outside the province. It is possible that they may have turned up here as strays but since specimens to authenticate the records are not known to exist, they cannot be included. Improper identifications are possible.

Polites baracoa (Lucas)   Baracoa Skipper

A subtropical species from Florida and Georgia which is included in several old lists. It seems very unlikely to have occurred here even as a stray and is more likely to have been the result of an improper identification.

Polites vibex (Geyer)   Whirlabout

A more southern species found in an old list under its former name of *T. brettus*. Its range is given as north to Connecticut. Klots quotes an old dubious record from Wisconsin while Forbes says that it strays to Toronto (!), possibly based on the above list. On the other hand, it is not inconceivable that it could stray as far as Ontario but without a specimen or more authentic record it must be considered doubtful.

Papilio kahli Chermock & Chermock   Kahli Swallowtail

A specimen in the Royal Ontario Museum labelled 'Cochrane' was originally thought to have come from Cochrane, Ontario. However, it was later determined that the label referred to Cochrane, Alberta. The species is known from central Manitoba and could conceivably be found in Ontario.

Phyciodes campestris (Behr)   Meadow Crescent

The recording of this species by Riotte from northwestern Ontario, is based on a genitalic examination of museum specimens. Riotte felt it might be only a variation of *P. batesii*; since its normal range is well to the west its occurrence is considered doubtful in Ontario.

Vanessa annabella (Field)   Western Painted Lady

One of the older lists records a single specimen of *V. carye* (its former name) from Toronto. The specimen is not now known to exist and the record is therefore considered doubtful.

BIBLIOGRAPHY

This listing contains the works consulted in the compilation of the records, timetables and other information.

1. **CHECK LISTS:**

Bailey, E.G., 1970; Butterflies of the Niagara Peninsula; Niagara Falls Nature Club.

Bethune, C.J.S., 1894; Butterflies of the Eastern Provinces of Canada; 25th Annual Rept. Ent. Soc. Ont. (1894): 29-44.

Bethune, C.J.S., 1896; Butterflies of the Eastern Provinces of Canada (Addendum); 27th Ann. Rept. Ent. Soc. Ont. (1896): 106-110.

Durden, C.J. & Dunlop, D.J., 1962 (Revised 1967); Checklist of the Butterflies of Algonquin Provincial Park; Park Museum; Ont. Dept. of Lands & Forests.

Eberlie, W.J.D., 1975; Annotated Checklist of the Butterflies of Northumberland County, Ontario; (Private Typescript).

Faull, J.H., 1913; Natural History of the Toronto Region - List of Butterflies; Canadian Institute, Toronto.

Fletcher, J., 1889; A Trip to Nepigon; 19th Ann. Rept. Ent. Soc. Ont. (1888); 74-88.

Gibson, A., 1910; A List of Butterflies Taken at Toronto; Ont. Nat. Sci. Bull.; 6:35-44.

Gregory, W.W., 1975; Checklist of the Butterflies & Skippers of Canada; Lyman Entomological Museum & Research Laboratory Memoir No. 3; Ste. Anne-de-Bellevue, P.Q.

Judd, W.W., 1963; Butterflies of Dunn Township; Ont. Field Biol.; 17:1-14.

Lamb, L., 1967; A Checklist of Waterloo County Lepidoptera, Papilionoidea; Kitchener-Waterloo Field Naturalists Conservation Committee.

Layberry, R.A., Lafontaine, J.D. & Hall, P.W., 1982; Butterflies of the Ottawa District; Trail and Landscape; 16(1): 3-59.

Lepidopterists' Society News; 1901-81 Annual Summaries for Zone 11.

Moore, H.K., 1962; Butterflies of the Milton Area; The Wood Duck - Hamilton Naturalists' Club; 15: 133-35.

McGugan, 1958; Forest Lepidoptera of Canada, Vol. 1; Dept. of Agriculture, Canada.

Riotte, J.C.E., 1959; Revision of C.J.S. Bethune's List of the Butterflies of the Eastern Provinces of Canada as far as Northern Ontario is Concerned; Ont. Field Biol.; 13: 1-18.

Riotte, J.C.E., 1971; Butterflies and Skippers of Northern Ontario; Mid-Continent Lepidoptera Series; 2(21): 1-20.

Riotte, J.C.E., 1972 (1973); On the Distribution of some Skippers in Ontario; Journ. Res. Lepid.; 11(2): 81-82.

Stewart, W.G., 1984; A List of the Butterflies of Elgin County, Ontario; (Private Typescript).

2. **TORONTO ENTOMOLOGISTS' ASSOCIATION:**

Catling, P.M. & Walker, C.H.; Annual Summary of the Rhopalocera Encountered in Ontario in 1969.

Catling, P.M., Edmonds, W.E.E. & Walker, C.H.; Annual Summary of the Papilionoidea & Hesperioidea Encountered in Ontario in 1970.

Catling, P.M. & Walker, C.H.; Annual Summary of Rhopalocera Encountered in Ontario in 1971.

Hess, Q.F.; Publication # 4-75 (Rev.) - Annual Summary of Rhopalocera in Ontario in 1972, 1973 and 1974.

Hess, Q.F. & Hanks, A.J.; Publication # 6-76 - Summary of Lepidoptera Encountered in Ontario in 1975.

Hess, Q.F., Plath Jr., W. & Hanks, A.J.; Publication # 7-77 - Summaries of Lepidoptera Encountered in Ontario in 1976.

Hess, Q.F. & Hanks, A.J.; Publication # 9-78 - Butterflies of Ontario & Summaries of Lepidoptera Encountered in Ontario in 1977.

Hess, Q.F. & Hanks, A.J.; Publication # 10-79 - Butterflies of Ontario & Summaries of Lepidoptera Encountered in Ontario in 1978.

Hess, Q.F. & Hanks, A.J.; Publication # 11-80 - Butterflies of Ontario & Summaries of Lepidoptera Encountered in Ontario in 1979.

Hess, Q.F. & Hanks, A.J.; Publication # 12-81 - Butterflies of Ontario & Summaries of Lepidoptera Encountered in Ontario in 1980, (ISBN # 0-921631-01-4).

Hess, Q.F. & Hanks, A.J.; Publication # 13-82 - Butterflies of Ontario & Summaries of Lepidoptera Encountered in Ontario in 1981, (ISSN # 0710-0574).

Hess, Q.F. & Hanks, A.J.; Publication # 14-83 - Butterflies of Ontario & Summaries of Lepidoptera Encountered in Ontario in 1982, (ISSN # 0710-0574).

Hess, Q.F. & Hanks, A.J.; Publication # 15-84 - Butterflies of Ontario & Summaries of Lepidoptera Encountered in Ontario in 1983, (ISBN # 0-921631-02-2).

Hess, Q.F. & Hanks, A.J.; Publication # 16-85 - Butterflies of Ontario & Summaries of Lepidoptera Encountered in Ontario in 1984, (ISBN # 0-921631-03-0).

Hess, Q.F. & Hanks, A.J.; Publication # 17-86 - Butterflies of Ontario & Summaries of Lepidoptera Encountered in Ontario in 1985, (ISBN # 0-921631-04-9).

Hess, Q.F. & Hanks, A.J.; Publication # 18-87 - Butterflies of Ontario & Summaries of Lepidoptera Encountered in Ontario in 1986, (ISBN # 0-921631-05-7).

Hess, Q.F. & Hanks, A.J.; Publication # 19-88 - Butterflies of Ontario & Summaries of Lepidoptera Encountered in Ontario in 1987, (ISBN # 0-921631-06-5).

Hess, Q.F. & Hanks, A.J.; Publication # 20-89 - Butterflies of Ontario & Summaries of Lepidoptera Encountered in Ontario in 1988, (ISBN # 0-921631-07-3).

Hess, Q.F. & Hanks, A.J.; Publication # 22-90 - Butterflies of Ontario & Summaries of Lepidoptera Encountered in Ontario in 1989, (ISBN # 0-921631-09-X).

Hess, Q.F. & Hanks, A.J.; Publication # 23-91 - Butterflies of Ontario & Summaries of Lepidoptera Encountered in Ontario in 1990, (ISBN # 0-921631-10-3)

Wormington, A., 1970; Butterflies of the Hamilton Area; The Wood Duck - Hamilton Naturalists' Club; 23: 64-65, 100-103.

Wormington, A., 1983; Annotated List of the Butterflies of Point Pelee National Park; Prepared for Parks Canada.

Wormington, A., 1989; Five Year (1984-1988) Supplement to the Butterflies of Point Pelee National Park, Ontario (1983), (ISBN # 0-921631-08-1)

3. GENERAL WORKS:

These works may be consulted for more detailed information on specific aspects of butterfly natural history.

Dos Passos, C.F., 1964; A Synonymic List of the Nearctic Rhopalocera; The Lepidopterists' Society; Memoir No. 1.

Edwards, W.H., 1868-1897; The Butterflies of North America - 3 Vols.; American Entomological Society, Boston, Mass.; Houghton-Mifflin.

Ehrlich, P.R. & Ehrlich, A.H., 1961; How to Know the Butterflies; Wm. C. Brown Co.; Dubuque, Iowa.

Ferris, Clifford D.,(Ed.), 1989; Supplement to a Catalogue/Checklist of the Butterflies of America North of Mexico; Lepidopterists' Society; Memoir No. 3.

Forbes, W.T.M., 1960; Lepidoptera of New York and Neighboring States; Cornell Univ. Agr. Exp. Stn., New York State College of Agriculture; Ithaca, New York.

Holland, W.J., 1930; The Butterfly Book; Doubleday & Co., New York.

Hooper, R.R., 1973; Butterflies of Saskatchewan; Dept. of Nat. Res. Saskatchewan

Howe, W.H., 1975; The Butterflies of North America; Doubleday & Co., New York.

Klassen, P., Westwood, A.R., Preston, W.B. & McKillop, W.B., 1989; The Butterflies of Manitoba; Manitoba Museum of Man & Nature; Winnipeg.

Klots, A.B., 1951; Field Guide to the Butterflies; Houghton-Mifflin Co.; Boston

Miller, L.D. & Brown, F.J., 1981; A Catalogue/Checklist of the Butterflies of America North of Mexico; Lepidopterists' Society; Memoir No. 2.

Moore, S., 1960; A Revised Annotated List of the Butterflies of Michigan; Museum of Zoology, University of Michigan; Ann Arbor, Michigan.

Morris, R.F., 1980; Butterflies and Moths of Newfoundland and Labrador; Publication 1691; Research Branch; Agriculture Canada.

Opler, P.A. & Krizek, G.O., 1984; Butterflies East of the Great Plains; The Johns Hopkins University Press; Baltimore.

Scott, J.A., 1979; Hibernal Diapause of North American Papilionoidea and Hesperioidea; Jour. Res. Lepid.; 18(3): 171-200.

Scott, J.A., 1986; The Butterflies of North America; Stanford University Press; Stanford, California.

Scudder, S.H., 1889; The Butterflies of the Eastern United States and Canada -3 Vols.;Cambridge, Mass.; The Author.

Shapiro, A.M., 1974; Butterflies and Skippers of New York State; Search 4: Cornell University; Ithaca, New York.

* * * * * * * * * * * * * * * * * *

PROVINCIAL RANKING OF STATUS

S1 - Critically imperilled because of extreme rarity (5 or fewer occurrences or very few remaining individuals) or because of some factor(s) making it especially vulnerable to extirpation

S2 - Imperilled because of rarity (6 to 20 occurrences or few remaining individuals) or because of some factor(s) making it very vulnerable to extirpation

S3 - Rare or uncommon (in the order of 21 to 100 occurrences)

S4 - Apparently secure, with many occurrences

S5 - Demonstrably secure and essentially ineradicable under present conditions

SN - Regularly occurring, usually migratory and typically non-breeding species for which no significant or effective habitat conservation measures can be taken; i.e., lepidoptera which regularly migrate to where they reproduce, but then completely die out every year with no return migration. Species in this category are so widely and unreliably distributed during migration that no small set of sites could be set aside with the hope of significantly furthering their conservation

Adapted from a report made to the Ontario Heritage Foundation by the Nature Conservancy of Canada.

* * * * * * * * * * * * * * * * * * *